THE COMPLETE
DEER STALKER

From Field to Larder

THE COMPLETE
DEER STALKER

From Field to Larder

Larry Fowles

THE CROWOOD PRESS

First published in 2021 by
The Crowood Press Ltd
Ramsbury, Marlborough
Wiltshire SN8 2HR

enquiries@crowood.com

www.crowood.com

British Library Cataloguing-in-Publication Data
A catalogue record for this book is available from the British Library.

ISBN 978 1 78500 854 2

Illustration credits
AnastasiaKopa/Shutterstock, p.146 (bottom); James Barron/Shutterstock, p.15 (top);
ATTILA Barsan/Shutterstock, p.38 (top); Paul Behan/Shutterstock, pp44 (bottom),
49 (bottom); Belizar/Shutterstock, p.57; Alexander Biggs/Shutterstock, p.61 (bottom);
Steve Bramall/Shutterstock, p.74 (middle); Callumrc/Shutterstock, p.68 (top);
John A Cameron/Shutterstock, p.41 (bottom); Designua/Shutterstock, p.60; Erni/
Shutterstock, pp52 (top), 55, 56 (top); Fisher Ltd UK, pp107, 112 (top and bottom);
Alexandr Junek Imaging/Shutterstock, p.42 (bottom); Martin Mecnarowski/Shutterstock,
p.45 (top); MilanB/Shutterstock, p.74 (bottom); Chris Moody/Shutterstock, pp45 (bottom),
74 (top); El Nariz/Shutterstock, p.119; Claire Norman/Shutterstock, p.14; PJ photography/
Shutterstock, p.37; Ondrej Prosicky/Shutterstock, p.91 (bottom); M. Rose/Shutterstock,
pp52 (bottom right), 54, 56 (bottom); SandersMeertinsPhotography/Shutterstock, p.50;
Paddy Scott/Shutterstock, p.17; Shaftinaction/Shutterstock, p.42 (top right); Shutterstock,
p.38 (middle left and middle right); Sandra Standbridge/Shutterstock, p.52 (middle left
and middle right); C.D. Strickland/Shutterstock, p.68 (bottom); George Trebinski, pp13,
24, 38 (bottom), 47, 48 (top and bottom), 71, 75, 81; Colin Robert Varndell/Shutterstock,
pp41 (top), 44 (top), 63; Karol Waszkiewicz/Shutterstock, p.45 (middle); WildMedia/
Shutterstock, p.42 (top left); Zacharie Studio/Shutterstock, p.113

Typeset by Jean Cussons Typesetting, Diss, Norfolk
Cover design by Blue Sunflower Creative
Printed and bound in India by Replika Press Pvt Ltd

Contents

Introduction

Deer hunting, indeed any form of hunting, is an emotive subject in the twenty-first century. Never before has this been the case, meat having historically been the 'best' food, demonstrated with numerous records of banquets with birds stuffed inside animals and lavish platters of game for lords and gentry, while poorer people ate vegetables and grain, supplemented with whatever fish, white meat or little red meat that could be obtained.

Venison, in having to be hunted, was the preserve of the very rich, as most others lived by subsistence farming. There simply wasn't time to hunt, even if land were available on which to do so. Such was the case throughout the medieval periods (AD425–1500) to the Tudor and Stuart eras. The Industrial Revolution in Georgian through to Victorian times meant a little leisure time for some, but meat was still a luxury. Slowly, perhaps since the end of World War I, diets included more meat, and different forms of hunting became available to the lower classes.

In recent times deer have multiplied rapidly and are now over abundant. They have no natural predators, and with the expansion of coppices, woods and forests in England (*see* Chapter 10), the deer's lot has been a happy one in recent decades. As a result, damage to tree and other crops is cited, as well as the cost to human life itself. The increased deer population has led to many deer crossing the country searching for food and quiet shelter, and accidents involving vehicles as they cross busy roads are rising – 400 to 700 people are injured, and sadly around twenty people a year die from deer-related collisions.[1] It is a fact that deer need to be controlled – that is, culled – in the UK in greater numbers than ever before.

However, cultural attitudes have changed considerably, and meat is no longer seen as an aspirational food source for many people. Deer culling is opposed by groups calling for alternative ways of controlling numbers. Arguments are put forward that deer management can be achieved through non-lethal means, which is true on a small scale. Often deer-proof 2m-high fences are erected around vulnerable woodlands, while individual saplings in smaller plantations can be protected with tubes around the young trunks. But countrywide, this has little effect on the deer population as a whole, as deer will simply move on to the next unprotected wood; it will not reduce their numbers. Covering all rural areas with plastic tubes and fences is not a practical solution.

Sterilization is one way of population control promoted by opponents to culling. Such programmes have been carried out in the United States on isolated populations, such as New York's Staten Island, an area of just 150sq km (58sq miles), with a population of around 2,000 deer in 2015. A $4.1million scheme sterilized 1,154 deer, reducing the population by just 8 per cent over three years. This will need constant attention however, such that a $2.5 million contract is being awarded to carry it forwards another five years. The cost was $3,727 (£2,900) per animal sterilized.[2] On that basis, Britain's estimated 1.5 to 2 million deer would require a sterilization programme that would cost eye-watering sums, even if it were possible to capture or get close enough to dart a good proportion of the female deer across open countryside and the hills of Scotland.

Perhaps in the future there may be a safe and effective contraception or sterilization method to control our wild deer population, but at present it is not even on the horizon. Cutting-edge research is exploring the insertion of immuno-contraception (IC) antigens into pollen or plant spores for example, but the questions of side effects and unintended consequences, if such a strategy proved remotely possible, need to be answered. It is a complex area, including the likely increased longevity of a female that does not produce young, and the effects on male deer puberty, antler growth and behaviour if males ingest a vaccine meant for females, among other issues.

Authorities and respected researchers both in this country and in others are of the consensus that immuno-contraception 'works very well when injected into female deer, but there are currently no delivery systems that can be used to implement IC in free-living, wild deer'.[3] The piecemeal management of our resident deer will need to continue, each landowner culling, or not, the deer roaming over their land as they see fit.

This book recognizes the increased population numbers of certain species, and the rapid changes in hunting technology, and discusses what this may mean for the stalker on his or her patch in the UK.

An inspector in the early 1960s, examining pig plucks. There is a long history of meat inspection in the UK.

ABOUT THE AUTHOR

I came into deer stalking along a fairly unusual route. I was employed in the red meat industry at the time as a slaughterman; the owner of the abattoir was a landowner and farmer. As a teen-

The author, working at an outdoor abattoir with reindeer. Near Gol, Norway, 1980.

ager I would work weekends, collecting hay and straw by small lorry and conveying it from the farm to the abattoir lairage. The farm connection developed into shooting rabbits and pigeons, which I would sell to local butchers. Later my interest turned to deer and because of the day job, carcasses posed little issue to me. I happily shot a few deer as the ground allowed, either for the farmer, the local butcher or myself.

Years later, without the old land I used to stalk, I went out for paid stalks with a professional in Dorset. We got along well, for he was an ex-meat industry worker too. I learned much from him, and the professional stalkers I've met since have been founts of knowledge as well, there for the asking.

A few years on, through red meat industry-related connections, I landed an informal, part-time job culling deer on an estate in Berkshire. The mid-1990s, although only some twenty-five years ago, were very different times compared to deer stalking today, and I was quickly approached to 'manage' the deer on two adjoining estates also. From the outset, my task was to reduce the populations to an acceptable level, as the deer had never been culled as part of a concerted management programme. The carcasses were sold to a dealer, with perhaps ten a year returned to the landowners. I still manage these three estates, along with a couple of smallholdings.

I have never been a trophy hunter, and I'm still not drawn to shooting specific deer because they have a large set of antlers on their heads: that concept is alien to me. Perhaps it's my background in the meat industry – each animal is primarily a source of meat. I do understand that for others, antlers are a big deal, but for me a buck or a stag is a bigger carcass and harder to drag back and lift into my truck!

My job at this time was as a meat inspector in various abattoirs, both large and small, inspecting carcasses for human consumption. Inspectors also oversaw animals prior to slaughter (ante-mortem), and ensured that slaughter was carried out in a humane manner. I was inspecting some 800 sheep each morning alongside four colleagues (deer are anatomically much like lean sheep, apart from not having a gall bladder), with perhaps 200 cattle later in the day. At other times I was at a pig plant, where the daily throughput was around 2,200 animals. This informed my deerstalking, such that a quick end to the deer's life and the full inspection and use of the carcass thereafter were of paramount importance.

Meat inspectors have an important role to play in overseeing safe meat production in this country, and the number of TB reactor cattle, for example, coming through one plant was astonishing, with lesions often found in places not normally associated with this classical disease. Applying this knowledge to deer carcasses, I admit to being surprised at the lack of understanding of many pathological conditions in deer by some UK deer stalkers, who are able to put small numbers of carcasses into the food chain without further checks.

To this end, this book is partly aimed at those hunters wishing to further their knowledge of the deer carcass, also to guide them in examining borderline cases, and judging when to pass as fit carcasses that might otherwise be unnecessarily thrown away. I have also learnt a lot in the field, both from my own observations and much more from others whom I have met along the way, and I am pleased to pass on all this acquired knowledge. I hope that the information contained in these chapters from my involvement in the much larger red meat trade (in the UK, some 540,000 animals are killed weekly, compared to 350,000 deer yearly)[4] will aid the stalker in processing his or her deer into venison in a humane and hygienic manner. This will, in turn, promote confidence in the methods of production and therefore the venison itself to the end user, the general public.

ACKNOWLEDGEMENTS

The chapter on deer senses was greatly informed by Professor George Gallagher and Assistant Professor Gino J. D'Angelo, both at the University of Georgia, USA. I thank them for their time and correspondence, and the use of their research.

I am especially pleased to share the images in Chapter 9 of various diseases and conditions, as they give another dimension to the written word. Some images are mine, but both David Barrah (senior meat inspector, retired, and part-time lecturer in comparative anatomy and disease at Bristol Veterinary School) and Dr Andrew Grist (lecturer at Bristol Veterinary School, and author of four meat inspection textbooks) have both generously given me permission to reproduce their images, and have amended some descriptions in the text.

No doubt some will disagree with me on certain aspects of my thoughts and observations, but putting forward ideas for debate is all to the good. Where relevant I have sought to justify my views, rather than state them as facts. As stalking deer is necessarily a solitary occupation, one can meet and discuss issues with only relatively few people, and one way of reaching a wider audience is with the old-fashioned book. This allows me to expand on a subject, and having put my name to it, I have sought to be unbiased and straightforward.

Chapter 1

UK Law Concerning Deer and Stalking

In England, Wales, Northern Ireland and Scotland, laws regarding the shooting of deer centre on welfare issues around the animal's yearly lifecycle and the humane killing of our six species. The lifecycle provisions address pregnant does in the run-up to birth and dependent fawns thereafter, while humane killing concerns the use of a suitable weapon with an expanding projectile (bullet) to ensure a quick death. Both of these areas are discussed below and in Chapters 2, 3 and 5.

From these come our basis for deer stalking, as opposed to the situation in some other countries, which have a government department that oversees deer populations. This department will issue licences or tags to shoot specific numbers within their seasons, as in the United States for example, which stipulates the deer to be taken on the large tracts of state-owned land. In the UK it is left to landowners and/or the holder of rights to manage deer numbers on privately owned land as they see fit. Only in Scotland has a government body occasionally stepped in to cull deer on specific estates on welfare grounds due to large populations not being managed effectively.

As the lifecycle of deer does not change year on year, the information below is unlikely to alter. However, populations grow and decline, technology changes, and materials are sometimes reclassed as hazardous. It is good practice to keep abreast of these changes by checking in with organizations such as the British Association for Shooting and Conservation[1] and the British Deer Society[2], for moratoriums due to extreme weather or disease control. This would include foot and mouth outbreaks, areas newly banning lead projectiles, and other changes that can be put into effect quickly, as would be the case if chronic wasting disease (*see* Chapter 9) were found in the deer population in this country.

CLOSE SEASONS AND TERMINOLOGY

The close season is the period in the year when it is illegal to shoot members of a certain sex of a deer species. We often speak of the doe and buck seasons, but these are catch-all terms, probably an Americanism that has taken hold in the UK. Red and sika male and female deer are properly called stags and hinds, and their young are known as calves. All other deer species are termed bucks, does and fawns.

Does and Hinds

The close season for the females of each species is set in order to safeguard their welfare during the last two months of pregnancy, through birth to the weaning of their young. For example, the roe doe open season finishes at the end of March, and they will give birth from late May through to mid-June. The young are said to be weaned by November, so the doe season opens on the first of that month, the rationale being that if the mother is shot, the fawns are able to fend for themselves.

There is, however, ongoing discussion about this, as some late-born fawns, particularly if they have a poor summer and autumn, may not be independent of their mother by the time the season opens. Similarly, the one month extension of the doe-stalking season to 31 March implemented in 2008 is distasteful to some, as the doe will be heavily pregnant by this time and although the foetus will not be viable (able to survive) outside the womb, it will be all but fully formed. *See* Chapter 6 for further discussion on this matter.

The doe seasons are a compromise between, on the one hand, having enough time to complete the required cull in reduced winter daylight and poor weather, and the animal's welfare on the other. The stalker who knows his ground and his deer well will be able to judge whether he can start his doe cull in November, and would hope to finish it by early March, if not sooner. It is best to work within the parameters of the deer seasons as enshrined in law, and not push them to the limit.

Bucks and Stags

Buck seasons concern sporting considerations, where antlers are a trophy, as much as anything else; thus bucks are out of season during the regrowth of their antlers.

Of course in order to gain an appreciation of the age and quality of a buck, you need to see the fully grown antlers. The resident stalker will again know his deer and will either cull or leave certain animals to breed, the aim being to improve the quality of bucks in his or her area. But aside from this, there is no physiological reason why bucks need a season. A minority consider that culling bucks while they are in rut is rather unfair; fallow, red and sika bucks in particular are full of testosterone at this time and are solely concerned with reproduction, so they become an easy target. This is quite apart from the fact that they lose much of their condition by not eating, and the carcass can be tainted with the smell of urine and testosterone: it is therefore

Table 1: Female Close Season

	England, Wales and N Ireland	Scotland
Red	1 April–31 October	16 Feb–20 October
Sika	1 April–31 October	16 Feb–20 October
Fallow	1 April–31 October	16 Feb–20 October
CWD	1 April–31 October	Not found in Scotland
Roe	1 April–31 October	1 April–20 October
Muntjac	No close season	

(CWD: Chinese water deer)

Table 2: Male Close Season

	England, Wales and N Ireland	Scotland
Red	1 May–31 July	21 Oct–30 Jun
Sika	1 May–31 July	21 Oct–30 Jun
Fallow	1 May–31 July	1 May–31 July
CWD	1 April–31 October	Not found in Scotland
Roe	1 November–31 March	21 October–31 March
Muntjac	No close season	

Notes on Deer Seasons

- In Northern Ireland only red, sika and fallow deer are found, but the law would apply equally there if other species were to become resident.
- Variations in the close seasons in Scotland arise due to weather conditions, which are invariably harsher than in southern England.
- Muntjac have no close season as they breed all year and do not have a specific rut period.
- Chinese water deer (CWD) have the same season for male and female, as they are extremely difficult to distinguish from each other; the blanket close season therefore protects the doe's late pregnancy through to weaning.
- Unlike small game, such as pheasants, partridge and hare for example, there are no restrictions to shooting deer on Sundays or certain public holidays. Deer can be shot on all days of the year, within their open seasons.

Deer antlers are a valuable trophy to many stalkers.

not the best venison for the table – but that is said with my meat inspector hat on.

LEGAL RIFLES FOR DEER

Further legislation covers the calibre of gun with which you are legally permitted to shoot deer. Long gone are the days when deer were commonly targeted with shotguns using no.6 shot in a drive along with pheasants. A shotgun can still be legally used, however, but in very restricted circumstances where serious damage can be proven, and using AAA shot or a minimum 350 grain rifled slug. This method is not discussed further here, as the use of a shotgun is very limited in scope and is viewed by most as an unsuitable weapon. Shooting with rifles of the legal calibre is the accepted way to deal with deer that are causing much damage to crops. The various terms and vagaries of this subject are contained in Chapter 2.

The Deer Act of 1991 stipulates that in England and Wales a minimum of .240 calibre with a muzzle energy (m/e) of not less than 1,700ft/lb is legal for all species of deer from muntjac to red, using expanding ammunition. No minimum bullet weight is specified, as attaining the m/e requirement requires a bullet of at least 85 grains in weight travelling at over 3,000ft/sec, for example. The heavier the bullet, the less hard it needs to be driven to exceed 1,700ft/lb.

Muntjac and Chinese water deer (CWD) can be shot with a smaller calibre, of not less than .220in and an m/e of at least 1,000ft/lb. A minimum bullet weight of 50 grains also applies, and must be of expanding construction.

In practical terms, stalkers generally have a minimum of the popular .243 chambered rifle, which covers the 1,700ft/lb requirement if the barrel is long enough. Some shorter barrels of around 50cm (20in) or less struggle to attain the velocity needed to satisfy the muzzle energy. While it is nice to use a lighter and handier .22 centre-fire rifle for muntjac and CWD, it is very restrictive and would be illegal to use if a larger species of deer crossed the stalker's path, which, invoking Murphy's law, is bound to happen!

In Scotland, the requirements are a little more specific. While a minimum calibre is not specified, a minimum muzzle energy of 1,750ft/lb, with a bullet weighing no less than 100 grains, together with a minimum muzzle velocity of 2,450ft/sec, is legal for all deer. However, roe can be taken with a minimum 50-grain bullet weight travelling at at least 2,450ft/sec and developing at least 1,000ft/lb of energy. In practice, this means the starting point for larger deer is again the .243 and .222 for roe, CWD and muntjac not found north of the border.

Northern Ireland, as noted above, has only the larger red, sika and fallow species. Across these, a minimum 100-grain bullet giving a 1,700ft/lb from a calibre not less than .236in is required. In practice a .243 is the minimum, the .236 stipulation being a technical way of describing the .240in minimum.

There is more information on calibres and bullets in Chapter 2.

LICENCES FOR OUT-OF-SEASON AND NIGHT SHOOTING

There is very limited scope for using special out-of-season and night-shooting licences, but before applying to Natural England, the Welsh Assembly Government or Scottish Natural Heritage to shoot out of season, the stalker should be aware that there are provisions in law for specific defences, if challenged.

The first is through section 7 of the Deer Act, which allows deer to be shot on welfare grounds. This would apply to a stalker shooting an injured deer, perhaps caught in a fence and unable to escape, or a deer wounded as a result of a vehicle collision, for example.

The second is the 'farmer's defence', where the owner of the land gives written permission for certain deer to be shot out of season to prevent damage, or further damage, to various crops, timber or other property on their land. As this is a defence, the onus is on the defendant — that is, the stalker and land owner — to prove that this was the case if they were prosecuted.

A licence to shoot out of season will only be granted in exceptional circumstances, and the protection of crops is not one of them. Valid reasons are to conserve natural heritage, and preserving public health or safety. These licences will only be granted when all alternative measures have been explored, such as fencing and day-time shooting, and will probably mean a visit from the appropriate authority to oversee the practices in place.

Night shooting is not permitted, except under special licence, defined as one hour after sunset to one hour before sunrise. This has particular relevance nowadays with various thermal devices; this is discussed in Chapter 10. Section 8 of the Deer Act allows a licence to be granted to shoot deer at night under similar conditions to section 7 — that is, conserving natural heritage, preserving public health and/or safety, and

Fallow does, just out of season but in the crop.

preventing damage to 'property' – that is, crops. Again there must be no practical alternative such as fencing or day shooting, which has to be shown to have been ineffective in dealing with the issue.

Note that a night-shooting licence does not allow shooting out of season, which is covered by section 7. However, section 7 does not allow night shooting, so effectively the shooting of deer both out of season and at night is never allowed.

SHOOTING AND THE PUBLIC

On our crowded island, bridleways and footpaths, often ancient rights of way, crisscross the countryside. On my permissions there are some six different bridleways and four footpaths, which dictate stalking activities to some extent. The general public have unrestricted access to these at all times, and the lone runner or dog walker will appear at any time, even on the most miserable, wet winter morning at first light!

The law states that no firearm should be discharged within 15 metres (50 feet) of the centre of a highway if it causes the user injury, or interrupts or interferes with their passage. This only applies to highways of vehicles, so shooting from and across footpaths and bridleways is permitted. It goes without saying that shooting near these areas requires utmost care, and if deer stalking is innocently disrupted by a horse rider, walker or whatever, that is part of the joys of hunting in this country.

However, the user of these paths should not loiter with the intent of disrupting the hunter's lawful activity, as this can then become trespass, even if they stay on the right of way. Deer stalking can be an emotive subject to some users of the countryside, but it is better not to have any confrontation, and to wait quietly for the person(s) to pass. If a conversation is inevitable, most people are polite when approached in a friendly and open manner, starting with a loud and cheery 'good morning', which helps to disarm walker(s) not fully on side. There is no point in talking in hushed tones at these times, as deer in the vicinity would already be well aware of people being present!

Walkers found well off the public right of way are, technically, guilty of civil trespass, but most are happy to be shown the footpath, especially when gently but firmly informed that shooting is being carried out in the area, and of the dangers it could cause them or their dogs. I believe that people discovered in this situation quietly know they shouldn't be there, and are therefore already on the back foot.

The law says that deer can be shot from a high seat, blind or on foot, but not from a vehicle unless it is stationary with the engine turned

Footpaths and bridleways.

Shooting deer from a vehicle is legal if it is stopped and the engine is switched off.

This doe expired across a boundary. Luckily I had permission to retrieve it.

off – a further public safety measure. Besides, it would not be at all easy to ensure a safe backstop and to check for stray members of the public while aiming at deer from a moving vehicle.

It is important to know that deer are not property, so are not owned by, and are not the responsibility of anyone. When on owned land, they become the property of that landowner when dead. If a deer is shot and then crosses a boundary and expires there, it belongs to that landowner. It is best to make contact with owners of land adjoining one's permissions well beforehand, to see how they feel about the possibility of recovering dead or wounded deer from their property. A text or phone call before you might need to do so would be appreciated, and keeps everything legal.

MAKING A START

For those wishing to explore deer stalking, the novice usually thinks of obtaining land to hunt over and the purchase of a firearm; however, this may not be necessary at first, or indeed at all, if all that was wanted was just the occasional stalk. Unless a person is really sure of his or her desire to stalk, or has prior experience, I would advise attending a course such as a Deer Stalk-

---

The Deer Stalking Certificate

The Deer Stalking Certificate (DSC) is a nationally recognized award, split between two levels. Level 1 gives general information about the six species and their identification, legislation, shooting and safety, and provides the required knowledge for carcass inspection, such that the successful candidate will be a 'trained hunter'. This is usually a three-day course with an assessment and a target-shooting test at the end.

Level 2 builds on the mainly classroom-based learning of Level 1, in that the candidate must demonstrate a deer stalk, the humane killing of the deer, then their ability to eviscerate, inspect and hygienically transport its carcass; this they must do on three separate occasions, overseen by an accredited witness. This can take some time to achieve, so a three-year period is allowed before re-registration is needed.

The DSC courses and awards are supported by the British Association for Shooting and Conservation (BASC), the British Deer Society (BDS) and the National Gamekeepers Association (NGO), and other rural agricultural colleges and commercial companies offer their courses and awards. All successful candidates are registered with Deer Management Qualifications (DMQ), a not-for-profit company that maintains the DSC certification, and quality assures the process. According to the DMQ website (dmq.org.uk), as of mid-2020 some 27,400 persons have completed the DSC Level 1, and 5,900 have completed Level 2, to give some idea of the uptake of the awards.

The DSC 2 isn't seen as a gold standard, but the foundation on which to build competence in the field.

ing Certificate Level 1 (DSC 1) (*see* box), which covers the basics of the sport – an overview in some respects.

Learning from a Professional

With an understanding gained from the basic course, the novice could then pay to go out with a professional stalker, using the provision in the law of an estate rifle. This allows a person without a firearms licence to use another's rifle while in their presence. Restrictions apply, but in practice this means the novice can be guided by the owner of the shooting rights of land over which they may shoot deer. This may satisfy the occasional deer stalker who wants just a few outings a year. He or she will have knowledge from the course, further enhanced by the professional, without the need to go through the process of applying for a rifle.

When I started in the 1980s it was much easier to obtain a firearms licence, but much of my practical knowledge came from a professional I went out with for some twelve days in total, spread over an extended period. One learns fieldcraft, riflecraft, as well as a host of other practical skills. I believe the money spent on those stalking days was worth every penny, and when I then stalked on my own permissions

I think I was fairly well prepared from the outset, instead of learning from the mistakes I could have made.

Target Shooting

The other route into stalking is via a target-shooting club; if successful in becoming a member, this will result in a firearms licence that allows a weapon to be shot, but only at an approved target-shooting ground. There are many clubs around the country, offering anything from an air rifle through .22 rimfire at 25 or 50yd (23 or 45m), to full-bore rifle shooting at 100m (109yd) and far beyond. A club will have an induction course, including safety on the range, and will introduce the novice shooter to a variety of club guns. Over time the probationary period will be met and the trainee's performance will satisfy the training officer, which may then help him or her obtain a firearms licence.

This is no overnight matter and will take some six months or longer, depending on the number of attendances. It must be said that target shooting in itself is an enjoyable and social activity. One may start with the ultimate intention of going deer stalking, but may be easily side tracked into entering the various competitions open to the target club member.

Learning with a professional stalker can teach the novice a great deal in a short space of time.

Regular shooting at a range gives familiarity and confidence in one's equipment.

The advantage of this route is that the trainee learns how to shoot accurately and safely, and gets to be at ease with his weapon as opposed to it being an alien tool. There is no substitute to spending time at the range, shooting perhaps thirty to fifty rounds at each visit in the case of a full bore, and more if a .22 rimfire gun. Much later, when the novice is finally faced with a shootable deer, familiarity with his or her rifle could be the difference between a successful hunt or otherwise, when the heart rate soars and one gets the adrenalin shakes while trying to be calm, called 'buck fever'.

A mentor may then take the novice along on his or her stalking trips as an observer, and/or the DSC 1 course could be taken. Subsequently, with suitable ground and police approval that they may shoot over it, the novice could apply to have his or her firearms licence endorsed so they are permitted to shoot deer, finally taking

to the field and shooting their first deer unaccompanied. Normally the police will allow a restricted licence, meaning that the rifle can be shot only over land approved by them, but this can be lifted after perhaps a year or two, allowing the licence holder to shoot wherever he or she has permission and judges the land to be suitable.

It can be a long process, but owning a firearm and being allowed to use it in the field is a responsibility. One's training helps prove the case for being licensed.

INSURANCE

Insurance is another area to cover before going out in the field, although it is not a legal requirement. We live in an increasingly litigious society, where we have to prove that our actions are lawful and correct, so being insured for third party accidents is a good start. Organizations such as the BASC, BDS or the NGO offer cost-effective group insurances for the amateur stalker.

Increasingly it is required to do a risk assessment, especially if a lease is taken from one of the larger landowners. It may take a few hours, but having this in writing shows that you have looked at the potential risks and have taken steps to eliminate or mitigate these to yourself and others. It is often surprising what comes up when thinking about potential situations. This goes hand-in-hand with the much maligned health and safety regulations, which requires that precautions are taken to avoid risks 'so far as is reasonably practical'; it is not to be viewed just as an exercise to cover the stalker from a lawsuit.

The HSE website[3] has much information on assessing the risks in the workplace, based around five points:

- Identify the hazards
- Decide who might be harmed and how
- Evaluate the risks and decide on precautions
- Record your significant findings
- Review your assessment and update if necessary

All this can be kept in a document and produced if the need arises, showing that the stalker has applied thought and care to their actions, ultimately demonstrating a good level of competence.

Identify the Hazards

Picking some brief examples, the 'hazards' could include coming across members of the public and local inhabitants while stalking. It is good to establish relations with people nearby, and they may be forewarned of your actions if you send a 'round robin' text to the estate workers and locals a day or two before your visit to the land, informing them of times and locations. If there is to be farm work in the area the stalker can in turn be informed, but mainly you can be reasonably assured that nobody should be in the vicinity, and if the hunter has a problem, those contacts will know where to look.

In certain woods, although there may be no public access, dog walkers often park their cars and frequent areas without thought of shooting activities, so staking 40 × 40cm signs at the access points warning of impending deer stalking that day is very useful in preventing a spoilt day. In a perfect world you wouldn't need to do this, but the 'right to roam' means different things to different people. Having done this, the stalker can show that he or she has mitigated the risk to others unknown to them, as far as is reasonably practical.

Most of the country has a phone signal nowadays, but if you are well off the beaten track trying to find a lost or injured stalker, the increasingly popular 'what3words' app on a mobile phone is extremely useful. Sent to the emergency services or another person, it pinpoints a 3 × 3m location, worldwide. Google maps is great for using postcodes while driving or walking, but cannot accurately locate a person in a remote wood as this app can.

IN CONCLUSION

Doing as much preparatory work as possible before a stalking foray will help to make the day

A simple sign, warning walkers of possible danger ahead.

run smoothly. If something goes wrong or the unexpected happens, the well prepared stalker will have a plan B as to someone to call, or perhaps an alternative way of completing the day. In the worst case scenario and police become involved, adherence to the law and being able to prove that one's actions were right and proper against hostile allegations may mean the difference between keeping or losing one's licence.

Deer stalking is often a frustrating form of recreation, and this should be impressed upon the novice from the outset. We all have stories of what could have been, but in the end there is always another day if you choose not to squeeze the trigger.

Chapter 2

Equipment

There is relatively little equipment that is absolutely necessary in order to stalk deer, just a loaded rifle, binoculars and a knife. But as in golf, although it would be possible to play eighteen holes with a single 6 iron, a variety of clubs and putters can help lower your score. Similarly with deer stalking, some additional equipment can increase the success rate, simplifying and aiding the process. What is important is to spend money on the right items, which I discuss in this chapter, ensuring years of trouble-free use without feeling the need to 'upgrade'.

OPTICS

Binoculars

The first item the hunter needs is relatively easy: a decent pair of binoculars, the rationale being that if you can't see the deer in the first place, it's going to be impossible to stalk it. This argument held good for many decades, but has softened a little in the last six years or so because of the thermal spotter – but more of this device later.

It was the case that binoculars from German or Austrian manufacturers stood head and shoulders above offerings from the Far East or America (often also made in the Far East and rebadged) in terms of quality, but the difference has narrowed considerably.

Choosing binoculars is a personal thing, in that what one perceives through the lenses may be different to another's experience. However, looking through a shop window in daylight is no test of their quality, and all binoculars will be able to give a good account of themselves from there. Borrowing a pair from a friend, or using a loan pair from a shop, will give a better indication of their ability to resolve images clearly when used at the cusp of darkness. Most stalking either starts or ends close to dawn or dusk, and the ability not only to distinguish but to positively identify deer from the similarly toned surrounding vegetation is crucial. These requirements will separate the best optics from the merely adequate. In southern England a pair of 7 or 8×42s is seen as a good compromise between usefulness in poor light and weight (*see* box).

Riflescopes

Scope choice mirrors the binocular discussion. The hunter needs a good rifle scope, for without it, he or she will not be able to see the deer that has been identified through binoculars. Although it is true that two generations ago deer stalking was carried out with open sights, technology has moved on and taken most stalkers with it. Again, German and Austrian scopes dominated the quality end of the market, with superb glass and very rugged construction. However, a host of manufacturers such as Minox, Vortex and Meopta, as

Binoculars with 32mm and 42mm lenses; the larger are better for dawn and dusk, but they are also heavier.

Scopes with 42mm fixed and 50mm zoom objective lenses; larger lenses are better for low light, but are mounted higher on the rifle.

well as the long-established American Leupold, produce excellent rifle scopes at around £1,000 and under. For many hunters, these optics are virtually indistinguishable from those costing upwards of £2,000, with good glass and the ability to withstand rough treatment, too. The high-end European manufacturers have countered by producing a more affordable line of scopes with fewer features, still with top quality glass, and these have sold well.

It used to be that a stalker put a 6×42 fixed magnification on his or her rifle in southern England, and perhaps an 8×56 for longer shots on the hill north of the border. The range of shots would be about 75m up to some 150m, and perhaps out to 250m on the more open ground in Scotland. But scope design has come a long way, and nearly all new scopes have variable magnification. The 3-12×50 seems to be the new norm, with 3-18×50 available from numerous brands.

Various forms of bullet drop compensation is now usually built in, such that a long shot at, say, 325m can be dialled in and the target aimed at precisely, rather than having to estimate holdover for the falling bullet at longer range. The old-school stalkers like to scoff at such advances, and no doubt a lot of venison is still put in the

Scope and Binocular Jargon

Binoculars with a designation of 7×50, for example, means 7× magnification; the 50 refers to the diameter of the objective (large, front) lens of the optic. This is important as it will indicate the size of the circle of light reaching the eye. This is found by dividing 50 by 7 = 7.14mm. The eyes of a person in their early twenties will have a maximum pupil diameter of around 7mm at dusk, so will be able to use all of the light reaching their retina. However, the maximum pupil size of someone in their mid-fifties, for example, will generally be smaller, perhaps 4.5 or 5mm across. That 7mm-diameter circle produced through the binocular will not be able to be fully used in this case, and the extra weight carried over a lighter pair of binoculars with smaller lenses will be wasted. Therefore 7 or 8×42s are seen as a good compromise between magnification, weight and light-gathering ability, aside from the quality of the lenses themselves.

Similarly, an 8×56 rifle scope is 8× magnification, 56mm front lens = 7mm dia. circle of light transmission, traditionally seen as a dusk or low-light lens. Issues develop when a higher magnification zoom lens is used at dusk. Take an 18× scope with a 50mm lens: just a 2.77mm diameter image is transmitted. That will produce a dim image in low light, maximum magnification being most useful during the day only, the zoom restricted to 8× or 10× at dawn or dusk to transmit a brighter image.

Roe buck at 163m (178yd) through an 18× scope.

chiller with simple but good quality fixed magnification scopes. However, the advantages gained with a scope having a large magnification range are many. A wide angle of view at lower magnification in the woods is best when shots can be at less than 60m. The stalker can them emerge into the open and at the far end of a very long field just prior to taking a shot, one can zoom on to a deer, initially spotted through binoculars, to verify if the roe buck is indeed a younger, shootable four-pointer, or a better buck that should be left for breeding stock.

Many of these scopes come with a fibre-optic red dot to help aim in very low light. I have mixed views on these. Most scopes I've reviewed have illumination, and they work well, but for me if it's too dark to shoot without the aid of the dot, then it's too late to shoot, period. If the shot at such an hour is less than perfect, the deer may well run off and be hard, if not impossible, to find in the darkness. I rarely use illumination for this reason; however, in a very dark wood with much overhead cover, a dot can be useful during the day.

THE RIFLE

The stalker is spoilt for choice here, as there isn't a new off-the-shelf rifle for sale in the UK that is actually bad, from the cheaper ones made in Eastern Europe, Turkey and the Far East, through American rifles, to the high-end German and Scandinavian manufacturers. Although there are a variety of designs, we are talking here of only the bolt-action rifle. A good 95 per cent of stalkers use this type because of its simplicity, reliability, potential accuracy and strength. Double rifles, for example, open like a shotgun to load two cartridges and are popular in Africa for a quick follow-up shot. However, they are shorter range weapons, and regulating the two barrels to shoot to the same point of aim beyond 100m is not easily achieved. They are usually more expensive compared to the bolt-action rifle. Semi-automatic full-bore (centrefire) rifles are not permitted in this country for deer stalking.

Back in 1957 the American writer Townsend Whelen wrote, among hundreds of other articles, a two-part piece often quoted, entitled

Making a Rifle More Accurate

A rifle in good general condition can often be made to shoot more accurately by machining and refining certain individual parts that have been made on a production line. The trigger can be honed so it breaks (fires) crisply, without creep and a spongy feel, aiding the rifleman's accuracy. The crown (the end of the barrel where the bullet exits) can be machined to be absolutely perpendicular to the barrel axis, ensuring the bullet leaves without catching on a minute burr or receiving a kick due to following gases escaping from one point in the circumference before another. The action and sometimes part of the barrel can be snugly bedded in the stock with epoxy, to ensure repeatable stability, shot after shot.

These relatively inexpensive gunsmithing improvements can be taken further by blueprinting, where the bolt is made to precisely match the action, and any flex or slack that can affect the accurate delivery of the bullet is removed. Alternatively a factory barrel may be removed and replaced with a custom barrel, perhaps of a heavier profile, which will have an accurately machined crown, the reason being that an existing barrel will become shot out (worn out) or pitted over time due to much use or poor maintenance. The action, in contrast, will not wear to any appreciable amount during normal use.

There are many good custom gunsmiths in this country who can take a professional look at a rifle and give an opinion as to what could and should be done. The shooting community is relatively small, and therefore poor advice is extremely uncommon from those in the gun trade, who have been in business for a number of years.

'Only accurate rifles are interesting'[1], the gist being that a shooter will lose interest if he is unable to improve his marksmanship due to poor intrinsic mechanical accuracy. This holds true today, and if you are unlucky enough to buy a rifle that doesn't shoot well after trying a variety of different ammunition, it can be very frustrating. The gunshop from where it came should be willing to investigate.

Almost any rifle, whether new or an older used one, can be made to shoot well with a little gunsmithing (*see* box), assuming that all the parts are in good condition – especially the barrel. It is important to buy a rifle that fits in order to get a good stock weld, which essentially means naturally mounting the gun in the same position each time to look through the scope, which should be mounted as closely as possible to the receiver, helping the accuracy potential of each shot. A good gunshop will offer guidance on this, so that each hunter finds their own 'best gun' based on price, style and fit, be it a walnut or carbon-fibre stock, stainless steel or blued action and barrel.

The import of this is that spending a lot of money does not guarantee a more accurate factory-produced rifle, there being little correlation between the cost and age of a rifle and its accuracy potential for the deer stalker. It can be demonstrated if a rifle shoots well by securing it with a vice on a bench at the range, then test firing it; if in the hands of the rifleman or woman the paper target cannot then be hit reliably, then it is they who need to improve their skills in marksmanship, and it is this which is more often than not the issue.

CALIBRE AND BULLETS

A great deal has been written in books and magazines about rifle calibres, and the subject continues to exercise hunters and target shooters on internet forums. To my mind these discussions of the merits of one calibre over another are, for the average novice or experienced deer stalker, largely unimportant. The law allows a .243 for shooting all deer in this country, big or small.

Apart from the two on the left (.22 centrefire, legal for smaller species, see text), all of these cartridges and many others in between are suitable for taking deer in the UK.

What is an Accurate Rifle?

A good standard to achieve is a three-shot group no more than 1in (25mm) apart, centre to centre, on a target at 100yd (91.5m), termed 1 MOA (see Ch 5). Purists will argue that at least five shots are needed for a proper group, but the stalker is only interested in where his or her first few bullets strike.

Many factory rifles are capable of better than this with selected ammunition, perhaps shooting a .5in (12.7mm) group. As the distances get longer the accurate rifle comes into its own, and at 300yd (274m), a very long shot on deer, it would produce a group of 1.5in, given that the rifleman does his or her part. The stalker would be well advised to keep hold of such a combination and concentrate instead on spending time in the field, knowing the rifle is well capable of doing whatever he demands of it.

The largest non-magnum calibre common in the UK is the 30-06, which is more than adequate for this purpose and also for most African, non-dangerous game. Virtually any calibre between these two will do the job, from the various 6.5mm offerings (the old 6.5×55 Swedish Mauser, and the newer .260 and 6.5 Creedmore), the 25-06 and .270, through to the equally old 7×57 German military round and the slightly larger .30 calibres, including probably the most popular and versatile of them all for the UK, the .308. All these, and many in between, are quite capable of humanely killing a deer at up to 300m (1,000ft).

Personally, I think the .243 is a little light for large fallow and reds at distance; however, many professional stalkers have shot a lot more deer than I have using this round. But perhaps that's the point: professional stalkers have the experience to place the bullet correctly so need less room for errors, which a larger calibre will give to some extent.

THE IMPORTANCE OF THE BULLET

All equipment discussed in this chapter is aiding one thing: the accurate delivery of the bullet, the only item that actually contacts and kills the deer. The construction of the bullet, if it hits the target correctly (*see* Chapter 5), largely determines if the deer dies quickly. An expanding bullet is necessary to hunt deer legally, but there are many types of these. One that expands rapidly upon impact and then disintegrates or separates may wound and only injure the deer superficially – this is often called a 'varmint' bullet and is produced for small, thin-skinned and light-boned animals such as foxes in the UK and prairie dogs in the USA. It is not suitable for deer. Conversely a harder bullet that only expands when bone is hit may pass between the ribs, through the soft tissues of the deer, and exit without deforming. This may not be immediately fatal, doing little initial damage and allowing the deer to run off, only to die later of slow blood loss.

A good bullet is somewhere in the middle, not too explosive and not too hard – a Goldilocks bullet. It will reliably expand to perhaps twice its original diameter whether it contacts soft tissue or bone, and no more. It will not disintegrate but will stay together, punching a decent-sized hole through the animal, destroying vital tissue along the way but not tearing a massive hole in the exit side of the animal, which leads to much meat loss at the larder. Such bullets are usually produced as a brand's premium bullet.

It is worth pausing for a moment to consider the construction of this vitally important item, weighing some 50 to 180 grains – that is, just 3.24 to 11.66g (grams), depending largely on calibre (*see* Chapter 1 for minimum bullet weights in different parts of the country for different species). Expanding bullets were all originally produced by stamping a copper 'cup', which forms the base and sides of the bullet; lead was then poured into the front void. When shot from a rifle at speed and on hitting the target, the soft lead at the front flattened against the harder copper base, thus expanding and doing more damage on the way through the animal than would be expected of its original size. However, the lead core of this older, simple design often separated from the surrounding metal, either meaning the bullet did not penetrate as required, or it split into many pieces, distributing lead throughout the strike area. Both scenarios are

not desirable, and deer thus shot may not die quickly from the shallow wounds inflicted.

Numerous more recent bullet designs aim to stop this separation, either by chemically bonding the lead to the copper base, or by crimping or sectioning off part of the bullet. Both methods work, but increase production costs. Personally I think the extra paid for premium bullets is absolutely worth the cost, even if 'standard' cup-and-core bullets only rarely fail to perform, as even just once is once too often. Further discussion of bullet choice can be found in Chapter 5.

A further point to consider is that certain bullets just do not shoot accurately in some rifles. My own Mauser seems to shoot flat-based bullets much more accurately than boat-tailed ones. Another rifle from the same manufacturer may do the opposite, and frustratingly it is a matter of trial and error, partly as a result of differing barrel harmonics.

Lead and Non-Toxic Alternatives

Lead in bullets is slowly becoming an issue, but lags behind shotgun cartridges in the use of alternative, less environmentally harmful metals. Lead is an excellent material for hunting bullets, being dense and therefore heavy, and easily moulded and deformed, as explained above. But having small shards of lead left in venison or in the ground is not desirable, so copper bullets are becoming more mainstream. They are designed somewhat differently in having petals that open on impact, causing a large wound channel but crucially staying together, leaving very little copper in the carcass. Some commercial leases now specify that only non-lead bullets may be used, and this is expected to become a norm in the future.

It seems sensible to me to prepare for this eventuality and experiment with copper bullets in one's own rifle to see what suits. I am currently doing just that, and if I am happy with the results I will not renew my favoured brand of lead-cored bullet heads once they are finished.

There could be an issue with copper and the .243 round. In Scotland a minimum 100-grain bullet is currently required, but copper, being less dense than lead, is longer for the same weight and will not meet that minimum weight in this smaller cartridge. Perhaps the law will be changed to accommodate this, but it may be that a slightly larger calibre will be necessary as a minimum in which to use copper bullets effectively.

Moderators

A moderator screws on the end of a rifle barrel, and is usually sleeved back over it to reduce overall length. The moderator *reduces* the noise of the firearm by slowing the gases released after the bullet has left the barrel, through a series of chambers. The sonic crack is not altered, as that is produced by the bullet being faster than the speed of sound, so bystanders are often surprised at the amount of noise emitted when a rifle is fired with a moderator fitted. The advice is that hearing protection should still be used, but for the few shots a stalker will make during a day out, most hunters do not. The moderator will reduce recoil and muzzle flip and may also aid

A .30-calibre 170-grain bullet recovered from a fallow, showing little expansion.

A recovered bonded bullet, with good expansion.

A .30-calibre 150-grain bullet; no bonding of lead can lead to separation.

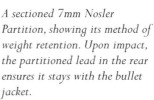

A sectioned 7mm Nosler Partition, showing its method of weight retention. Upon impact, the partitioned lead in the rear ensures it stays with the bullet jacket.

Numbers and Calibres

The different ways of describing a calibre can be confusing. There are two ways of naming a cartridge: the European way gives the diameter and the length of the cartridge case in millimetres: in the example 7×57 the bullet diameter is 7mm, and the case length 57mm. This is simple, and gives some indication of the capabilities of the round: for example a 7×64 cartridge uses the same 7mm diameter bullet as the first example, but in a longer case, therefore allowing more powder to be used, making it a more powerful round.

The American method often describes only the diameter in inches: thus .243 is the diameter of the bullet, and there is no information about the cartridge. Sometimes this is further complicated by historical information, such as, for example, the 30-06: this is a .30 diameter bullet, and the round first described in the year 1906, hence the -06 at the end. The 30-30, an old but still popular round, uses a .30in-diameter bullet again but the -30 part indicates that 30 grains of smokeless powder was used! The 25-06 shows that the bullet is .25in in diameter, while the -06 tells us that the parent cartridge was a 30-06, necked down to accept a smaller bullet. Often with American-style nomenclature, one really has to be familiar with the round to understand where it sits in the vast range of cartridges developed over the years.

For those wishing to dive into the large pool of reloading, the novice should be aware that it is almost a hobby in its own right. It is satisfying to hunt with home-loaded, bespoke ammunition finely tuned to your rifle, but for the average stalker taking eight or ten deer a year, the cost savings will not materialize for many years, if ever, over factory-produced ammunition. Further, commercially produced cartridges are now of a very high and consistent quality, reducing further the reasons to handload.

accuracy, but not in all cases. Although not a recent invention, being patented in 1909 in the States, moderators didn't become widely accepted in the UK until the late 1990s. Police forces didn't like to approve them, but somewhere along the line this was objected to on health and safety grounds, which cited that hearing would be affected without one fitted – and the police relented.

I have a copy of a letter I sent to the landowner of my permission asking if he minded if I had a moderator fitted to my rifle. Times have changed in a little over twenty years, and most stalkers now have one fitted as a matter of course; the reduced noise of a rifle with a moderator also helps to lessen the chance of spooking the deer, often enabling the stalker to get off a second shot at another deer.

It must be noted that a moderator needs to be applied for on a firearms certificate (FAC), as a rifle would be, which seems bizarre as it is an inert piece of equipment – but that's the law. Further, if taking the firearm abroad, some countries will not allow these devices to be used. Care must be taken to re-zero the rifle in this case, as using a moderator will usually significantly alter the point of aim.

SECURITY

Firearms and ammunition should be stored securely and separately when not in use, to the satisfaction of the local police force. The easiest way is to purchase an approved gunsafe, which is then bolted to a structural wall of the building. There are other ways of storage, depending on living arrangements, from a unit bolted to wooden rafters in the loft, to a purpose-built gunroom. It is best to ask the local firearms officer what they would like to see prior to purchasing, together with extra security arrangements for the premises if deemed necessary.

The only thing I would suggest on this subject is to buy or build a somewhat larger safe storage than might be required at the outset. Rifles, moderators and ammunition seem to multiply over the years, so it is better to allow for this from the beginning.

SHOOTING STICKS

The old Wild West films propagate a lie, the average shooter cannot aim his or her rifle accurately from the shoulder at medium, let alone long

Simple hazel rifle support.

Split sticks give better support than a single pole: more legs equal better stability.

A tripod gives single-point stability for the rifle.

Stalker with four-legged sticks and a roe sack over their shoulder.

range as often portrayed. Stalkers traditionally used a straight hazel stick with a V-shaped stag horn or with a branch off at the top in which to settle the gun as an aid to accuracy. Over the years stalkers progressed from that single stick to crossed sticks for more lateral control. Then tripods became popular, the rifle cradled from a single point on a lockable gimble. Then from around 2015, the so-called four-legged sticks became de rigeur, which actually have two points of contact with the ground but are split to give the rifle a stable platform fore and aft, giving lateral as well as vertical stability.

For longer shots the tripod and four-legged sticks are invaluable; on a calm day and with unstressed deer, it is possible to shoot fallow to 200m (218yd) with these supports, given practice. I would not attempt this with simple crossed sticks; perhaps shooting to 140m (153yd) would be my personal maximum. Any further and I would wish to get down and shoot prone, using a bipod attached to the rifle's fore stock, if the height of surrounding vegetation allowed. The various three- or four-legged sticks are well designed and can be used as quickly as a single stick in a hurry – but best of all one doesn't need the bipod; for me it has become redundant except at the range, so some weight can be saved while stalking.

A RANGEFINDER

In later chapters the rising fallow deer population across the UK is discussed. These are wary deer and difficult to approach. The cosy image of the southern UK deer stalker going out for a roe doe or buck in the local fields and woods is not such a representative idea nowadays. Living in herds, many eyes keep constant watch, and fallow are off and running at the slightest unusual movement. Longer-range shots are now more commonplace because of this, and a rangefinder then becomes a very useful tool. If the hunter estimates a fallow to be 200m (218yd) away, but it is in fact closer to 250m (274yd) away, the fall of a bullet over that extra distance could well make the difference between a good or a poor shot: hence the usefulness of the laser rangefinder. Available from about £140 upwards, these small pocket-

Leica 8×42 rangefinder binoculars: two instruments in one package.

able units typically measure to 400m (440yd), or up to 2,000m (2,200yd) in the more expensive, powerful models. The stalker, having 'pinged' the deer, can then decide whether to take his shot, or to move closer.

A fairly recent development is range-finding binoculars: the stalker is already looking at deer through binoculars, and a push on a button can give him the range while still looking through them, which instantly informs his or her decisions. This avoids having to fish around in your pockets to retrieve the little rangefinder. Costing upwards of £1,600, many stalkers have moved over to these combined devices to aid their shots, and having an all-in-one tool also saves weight.

KNIVES

After a successful stalk, the deer needs to be dealt with fairly rapidly. The hunter always carries a knife, often two, to bleed and eviscerate the carcass. Coming from a meat industry background, I have not been overly drawn to the available expensive custom knives. Certainly there is nothing wrong with paying hundreds of pounds for a fine handmade knife, but to me they are more works of art than a tool.

In the abattoir or butcher's shop you will find rather ordinary Victorinox, Swibo or Dick knives (amongst others) with a standard Fibrox handle, the 6 or 7in boning knife being widely used. These cost just some £12 each when bought in bulk. If there were a better option, you can be sure that tradesmen would buy such tools. The reason these are found industry wide is, in large part, the nature of the steel used. Expensive custom or high-end production knives use very stiff exotic steels, often laminated, hardened to 61 or 62 Rockwell (a measure of a material's hardness: the higher the number, the harder the material). The butcher's knife is of a thin, flexible, softer steel, at around 56 Rockwell. This will allow it to bend and flex around hide, joints and bone, feeling lively to the user, while the stiffer steels feel a little 'dead' in the hand.

It is true that the steel used for the more expensive knife will hold a sharp edge for a longer time in use. But once gone, it takes some effort to regain the edge, while the cheaper steel's edge will (almost microscopically) roll over, being soft and more malleable. A few simple strokes on a sharpening steel will realign the edge, allowing the user to carry on with a now restored, sharp blade.

Perhaps this is of no consequence to the stalker, who will only have to deal with a couple of carcasses at most at any one time, so one knife will see him or her through to the larder without re-sharpening. But I prefer a cheaper, fixed blade such as a Mora or folder, especially as it's not unknown for knives to be lost in the field during use!

A further point to consider is that the very sharp edge attainable with an expensive knife – as is often demonstrated by effortlessly cutting strips of paper, for example – may be too fine for the job; a toothier edge on a cheaper knife maintained with a steel could well be better suited for

A 6in boning knife, a 4in sheath knife and a folder, together with a sharpening steel, are all the stalker needs.

the relatively indelicate work of breaking down a carcass.

THE THERMAL IMAGER

Before discussing the equipment that is needed after the deer is shot, the thermal imager is the one recent development that is absolutely revolutionizing the way we stalk. Developed by the military in the 1960s for conducting operations at night, it works by picking up the heat emitted from a living being and differentiating the 'hot' body heat against the surrounding 'cool', shown on a small LED screen viewed through an eyepiece, rather like a digital camera. The civilian version can be used at any time of the day or night; during the hours of darkness, for example, a deer census can be carried out without needing to use spotlights, which would disturb the herds.

During the day in the woods, in cover or even across open fields, deer can be difficult to spot with binoculars. Stalkers have traditionally spent many hours glassing the ground in front of them, looking for a flicking ear or twitching tail amongst the vegetation. However, with the hand-held thermal imager, one sweep will show any living creature within a thousand metres or more, provided the heat signature isn't hidden behind thick vegetation. If an animal's thermal image shows, the stalker can then switch to his binoculars, and knowing where to look, can identify it.

With just a little experience it is possible to tell a small deer from a fox from the size and shape of the heat source. With the newer, more detailed imagers one can tell if a deer has antlers, so whether it is a male or female. With my simple imager I have found I can cover ground relatively quickly, knowing that if a deer is there I won't miss it. As a culling tool it is invaluable; however, as an aid to stalking as a sport it raises some larger ethical issues (discussed in Chapter 10).

EXTRACTING AND LIFTING CARCASSES

For the three larger species (fallow, sika and especially red), extraction after shooting can pose

A dead fallow in the centre of the image at 109m (119yd); it is not easily seen with the naked eye.

An iPhone shot, taken through an imager eyepiece. The dead deer in the photo at 109m (119yd) is very visible, even in this low quality image.

A quad bike is ideal for picking up larger animals, as it leaves little damage on soft ground.

logistical problems; however, with some planning, these can be minimized. Getting a carcass to a vehicle pick-up point might mean a 400 or 500m (440 or 550yd) drag even in the south of the country, which can be tough going, especially if it is at all uphill. This will detract from the day's enjoyment.

A harness of some sort can spread the load, as can a steel hook with two ropes attached, for dragging by two people. A drag sled can work on some terrain, especially if the ground is wet and soft, and will also protect the carcass from contamination. Some stalkers carry a rolled-up drag mat or wear a roe sack over their shoulders, so there is no need to trek back to the vehicle and back again to the carcass with the necessary items. The smaller roe deer will fit in a sack and can be carried over the shoulder, or it can easily be dragged, as it is just a third of the weight of a mature fallow. Muntjac and Chinese water deer are smaller again so pose no problems, and if the back legs are hocked they can be carried a long distance without effort, the front legs and nose just brushing the ground.

Many stalkers or syndicates with large tracts of land to cover use a quad bike for extraction. Even the smaller adult-sized machines make light work of larger deer carcasses. If many deer are to be culled, a quad can greatly ease the burden, as you can be sure of finding a shootable animal to cull at the furthest point possible from a track! Carcasses can be loaded on to a larger machine, or simply towed behind in a trailer, or dragged on a sled.

A wheelbarrow makes fallow easy to transport and keeps the carcass clear of contamination.

ANCILLARY EQUIPMENT

Inside the vehicle the stalker will keep a variety of other items, all useful at some point of the year. Such equipment would include larger 15cm (6in) knives and a sharpening steel; bags and strong compactor sacks for heads, feet and intestines; extra nitrile gloves; a small towel; bottles of water for cleaning the inside of carcasses and your hands; and a lamping kit in case of a night-time search or if illumination is needed. Packing extra clothing to change into should you get caught in a downpour is a good idea. A couple of tow ropes with shackles in case the vehicle gets stuck, a folding spade for burial, secateurs and a small woodsaw completes the container.

I have had a high-sided, removable, heavy-duty rigid plastic tray made that fits in the back of my vehicle, into which I lower the carcasses from a pulley arrangement fixed to the roof bar. This is waterproof and slides out for easy clean-

This nice four-pointed roe buck is easily dragged along the track.

ing and drying. It didn't cost a lot, but has been invaluable over the years.

This takes care of items that are not immediately necessary, but there is more to carry in pockets or a small rucksack when on foot. Personally I take seven extra rounds in a pouch – with four in the rifle this makes eleven in total; two knives; four pairs of blue nitrile gloves for evisceration and marking a position – one tied to a branch can be seen from a distance; a mobile phone; a head torch if on an evening stalk; and rope for dragging. In summer I like to take a bottle of water with me, even if I'm a maximum of forty-five minutes from the truck. I am

A simple hoist takes care of lifting a heavy carcass into the waterproof tray.

normally on familiar ground, so do not need a compass or a map.

CLOTHING

I don't wear camouflage while stalking. This is for two reasons: first, my stalking takes place near a market town, which I frequent for diesel and sandwiches, and cammo is never a 'good look' in urban environments. Second, I am yet to be convinced of its benefits for stalking deer. Camouflage was originally developed to try to hide humans and equipment from other humans, and it certainly works, but deer have eyesight that differs from ours (*see* Chapter 4). Movement is more of an issue when approaching deer, so my clothing just tends to be a drab green or brown.

There are a variety of hiking stores in the UK, and shirts, fleeces and gloves can be purchased from these establishments. Hiking has become 'high tech', with all sorts of innovative materials, and it is not necessary to keep buying traditional waxed cotton if something better is available. I do wear country-style moleskin trousers, as they work well in protecting from bramble, but as long as items are quiet in use and dull in colour, anything else goes.

We have mild winters in southern England, so heavy coats are largely unnecessary, and I can often go through a whole doe season with just a brushed flannel shirt and a windproof fleece, unless I am spending time in a high seat, which can get especially cold, sitting still for some hours. I favour a tubular face veil from a ski shop, and a brimmed hat to put my white face in shadow. A stalker should always wear gloves, even in summer, as hands give deer a chance to see movement against the darker background provided by the rest of the clothing.

For footwear, 80 per cent of the time low hiking-style boots suit best. Having had some cheaper pairs that were only waterproof for a few months at best, I feel that spending upwards of £200 on a good pair is economical over time. I wear these boots even in the warm summer months, as trainers cannot protect against twisted ankles that may occur on the uneven terrain the stalker will experience. Neoprene-lined Wellington boots have their place in the wet winter months, too. I prefer the ones with the firmer soles, which seem to have more ankle support. They are great in bramble, as not having laces and eyelets they don't get caught up as much as hiking boots. Another plus for Wellington boots is extra protection from ticks, which easily crawl up trouser legs when wearing hiking boots, unless gaiters are worn.

As for waterproofs, I find stalking in the wet a pointless exercise on my permissions. The deer hunker down, only jumping up and running off when you are really close by. Waterproof trousers can, however, be useful after a shower when stalking through wet undergrowth.

Chapter 3

Deer Species in the UK

This chapter outlines the six species of deer found in the UK. The overview will inform and allow the stalker to appreciate the differences between the species at various times of the year. An attentive hunter will note further differences to the general behavioural pattern in their own locality, which will add to his or her personal knowledge of the various species. My own area, for example, is very sensitive to muntjac. As soon as the population expanded we lost many roe; however, these made a comeback once a shoot-on-sight muntjac policy was implemented. In another local anomaly, the foetuses recovered from fallow does over the years showed that as many as one in three were carrying twins, a normally more rare event.

ROE DEER

Roe are one of two truly native species of deer in the UK, the other being the red, archaeologists having found evidence of their presence since the Mesolithic period, 6,000 to 10,000 years ago. Larger than muntjac and Chinese water deer, does stand up to 77cm (30in) at the shoulder, with the bucks only a little bigger. Weighing in at 15 to 30kg (33 to 66lb) live, a mature doe in good condition can reach around 17kg (36–38lb) dressed for the chiller (that is, with the head and feet off at the hocks, and the body cavity empty), and bucks slightly more at around 18kg (38–42lb) in southern England.

According to recent censuses[1], roe are the most widespread of our deer, reaching all parts of the UK except eastern Wales, and highly urban areas such as the Midlands and London. Roe are very adaptable and can thrive in both broadleaf and conifer woods, as well as along hedgerows,

in small coppices, on moorland and even in large gardens. They eat a wide variety of shrubs, the buds and leaves of trees, young bramble, acorns, heather, ivy, herbs and ferns. They are picky eaters however, preferring the younger, tender tips of the various greenery available, so they can do much damage browsing in this way, even though they do not consume as much as the larger species of deer.

Identification

The roe's pelage goes through a number of changes through the year. In summer it is a rich reddish brown, turning to a dull, darker grey in

Note the pearling on this mature six-pointed buck's antlers. Pearling starts to disappear as the buck goes past his prime.

Note the difference between the downward-pointing rump tush of the does and the smaller, kidney-shaped buck rump patch. This is February or early March, still with a silvery grey winter coat.

Mature roe buck in full, rich, chestnut-red summer coat.

Young roe buck in spring, looking scruffy while losing his winter coat.

Summer-coated doe and yearling fawn / kid, which has a noticeably shorter muzzle.

winter, with a white rump. In spring the coat looks very shabby, as the winter grey is shed in clumps, with the summer coat showing through beneath. The kids (occasionally also called fawns) are darker, with spots that fade before the first winter.

Characteristically roe have a black nose, a white chin and a rump patch. The doe has a tush, a downward-pointing tuft of hair which can look like a short tail. The rump patch aids in differentiating the sexes: that of the doe covers a larger area than the buck's, which will be kidney-shaped and more yellow-white in colour. When roe are alarmed, the rump patches of both buck and doe flare, having erectile hair, and both sexes utter a single bark, repeated regularly, or two or three barks as they bound away. Kids make high-pitched squeaks, to which the doe will reply with a stronger squeak.

Roe do not form large herds like fallow, but groups of twelve to fifteen are not uncommon, especially with kids in tow in late summer, when they can be seen feeding and playing on open stubble.

Roe are territorial deer, especially the bucks from March to the rut ending in August, during which time they will chase away other bucks straying on to their patch. This makes life a little easier for the stalker, as the location of roe can then be better relied upon once known. Unless really hassled, roe are relatively tolerant of nearby humans; even when one of a group is shot, the others may not go far, and the younger ones can return to the scene after some ten minutes. Together, this makes it easier to stalk roe and to achieve a planned cull compared to other deer species, which will leave the area for weeks at a time if overly stalked.

The Roe Year

The rut runs from mid-July to mid-August, when the doe becomes fertilized; however, the egg does not start to develop for some four or five months due to delayed implantation. The species developed this unique technique to avoid giving birth in the colder months; being born in May/June, the young then have the maximum chance of survival. This also places less demand on the doe's body during autumn and early winter,

enabling the female to build reserves, in the form of fat, to then use in later winter. Usually twin kids are born from mid-May to early June. A single kid may be produced in the doe's early years, and triplets are not rare if conditions are good.

The kids are left alone by the mother for the first few days, hidden in undergrowth, and she returns only to suckle them. They do not have a scent so are not easily found by the fox, their only natural predator now Britain has no wolves and lynx. Farm machinery probably accounts for many more kid deaths than the fox, as they fall victim when grass is cut for silage during warm weather.

Only a few days after birth the young are up and following the mother, so during the harvest in August to early September a relatively small window of opportunity to count numbers presents itself as they forage on the cut fields. However, stubble is rapidly ploughed in these days, so the deer have little reason to be out in the open.

Antler Development

Roe buck antler growth differs from other deer species. Antlers are shed in November/December, those of the older bucks first, but start to regrow almost immediately. Fully developed by April, the velvet dries and is rubbed off against flexible young trees and saplings. This brings the deer into conflict with foresters and landowners, who don't appreciate the bark being removed from their crop as it stunts and deforms later growth, and sometimes kills off saplings altogether.

The roe buck kid will develop small buttons on their pedicles, which shed in spring the year following birth. Proper antlers then grow yearly, with the first at two years being single spikes of about 10cm (4in) in length. The three-year-old has two points on each antler (a four-pointer), while a four-year-old has six points in total. However, in good feeding areas the yearling can have four points and a three-year-old can easily have six. In subsequent years the antlers become thicker, with pearling around the coronets, which may fuse together.

At seven or eight years the buck starts to 'go

back', being past its prime; it probably lives to ten years in the milder climate of southern England. Signs of an older buck would be a decrease in pearling, coronets that appear to slant, and its back would no longer be straight, but would dip a little along what would be the saddle.

Roe Stalking

The stalking season follows the doe cycle, so the season opens on 1 November, kids being broadly independent by this time, although it is possible to see kids still feeding from the doe until the New Year in some cases. The season ends on 31 March, which for some is too close to the birth of the young, the foetus being all but fully developed. There have been calls for the re-introduction of the shorter doe season of 1 November to 28 February, as it was before 2007, but with the spread and increase in the overall population this is unlikely unless numbers decline. (*See* Chapter 6 for more on this subject.)

The buck season follows sporting considerations, so roebucks are out of season during the shedding and regrowth of their antlers. When the season opens on 1 April the younger bucks are still in velvet, but the older animals will be mostly clean. The season ends on 31 October, just before shedding commences. Over the winter, antler-less bucks are not appreciably different in size from does, and when the stalker is identifying the intended shot, he or she needs to take a close look for pedicles, a penile sheath – or just how the deer urinates – and the shape of the rump patch with a tush to ensure that the right sex is taken.

RED DEER

The red deer is one of the two native species in the UK (along with roe), having migrated from Europe 11,000 years ago. These deer thrived in the then forested and sparsely populated British Isles for some 4,000 years. Since that time the red has not always had an easy time here. From c.4000 to 2500BC the gradual increase in settlements and areas cleared for farming made for an ever-declining red population.

From 1066, the Normans kept deer parks and forests specifically for deer hunting for 100 years, but after that, during the late medieval period, red numbers declined. Eventually the population was confined to just the Scottish Highlands, the south-west of England and a few other smaller pockets. In the nineteenth century efforts were made to re-establish the red by cross-breeding with the larger wapati and introducing the species into other areas. In the late twentieth century, increasing areas of forest countrywide has been a boon to red deer, which are now expanding in numbers and range due to the underculling of does and the colonizing of large plantations north of the Scottish border.

The red is the largest deer in the UK, the stags standing up to 137cm (54in) at the shoulder, and the females up to 122cm (48in). In southern England the average weight for a strong stag would be about 180kg (400lb) and 120kg (260lb) for a hind. Hill reds in Scotland are smaller due to the harsher weather conditions and poorer feeding, being some 90kg and 65kg (198lb and 143lb), respectively. Back at the larder, a good southern stag will be around 95kg (210lb) in the skin, and a hind around 60kg (130lb).

The red prefers the forests and woodland in England and southern Scotland, but adapts readily to open hills and moorland. These deer will eat dwarf shrubs, grasses, heather and tree shoots, but also agricultural crops, which puts them in conflict with farmers and foresters. As big animals, they can eat much vegetation and cause considerable damage.

Identification

The red has, unsurprisingly, a reddish-brown pelage in summer, fading to a grey brown in winter. They do not have spots as mature animals; calves are born with spots but lose them by eight months of age. The rump patch is a most distinctive feature, creamy in colour and extending up and over the back. It is not outlined by a black line, as is that of the fallow or some sika. Red deer stay in single-sex herds until the rut, when the stag will typically roar to assert his position; hinds emit a deep bark when alarmed, but moo in a somewhat cow-like manner when looking for their calves, which bleat back. Come autumn, stags will grow a mane, which they keep over the winter.

The Red Year

The rut starts at the end of September, continuing through to November. Mature stags leave their single-sex groups to seek and defend a group of hinds, typically ten to fifteen in number, but occasionally many more than this. Defending their group from other stags is achieved by roaring contests, parallel walking and the locking of antlers. After a gestation of 240 to 262 days a single calf (occasionally twins) is born from mid-May, with peak births in the first two weeks of June. The calf is weaned at four months, but may suckle for longer. Woodland hinds can breed at sixteen months, but hill reds do not mature so quickly, being initially fertile at just over two or three years of age. Furthermore, hill hinds may not produce a calf every year, as will their better fed cousins in the south. A mature hind that doesn't produce a calf is called a yeld.

The open season for hinds in England, Wales and Northern Ireland is from 1 November to 31 March; for stags it is 1 August to 30 April. Scotland has an earlier and shorter season for hinds, from 21 October to 15 February, while Scottish stags may be taken from 1 July to 20 October only.

These dates, as with the majority of other UK deer, follow the yearly female cycle, so the season is closed from when the does are in late pregnancy until the calves are independent. Stags are in season when the antlers are clean of velvet, so sporting considerations prevail here. However, after the rut the red stag may well be in poor condition, having expended much energy and not eaten for some time, so the carcass is not good for the table; this ties in with the close season for Scottish stags.

Antlers

Red stags are prized for their antlers, which will reach their peak when the stag is between eight to twelve years old. A calf's pedicles will develop during the first winter. The yearling will then grow bony knobs over the following summer, perhaps long spikes if the feeding is

Winter-coated red hind in spring.

Younger red stag (staggie) with six points and a winter mane.

Red hind in summer coat with her calf; note the spots.

Mature red stag in summer coat; a red stag has no mane at this time of the year.

BELOW: *Red hinds with their summer pelage coming through the winter coat. The rump patch comes up over the back.*

good; they will be clean of velvet by September. In the lowlands or in south-west England, bigger heads on yearlings are not uncommon. The older stags cast and regrow their antlers, and are clean of velvet (in 'hard horn'), before the younger animals.

The antlers develop each year to a peak of a classic 'royal', which has six points on each antler, made up of brow, bey and trey tines with a 'crown' of three points at the top. Park or woodland deer that are well fed and not stressed, may have many more points than this. Thereafter, the older stag will have successively lesser heads, where the lower portion carries less weight and the points are shorter and more spindly, collectively this is termed 'going back'. Occasionally a stag may not grow antlers at all. This is possibly due to poor nutrition just as the pedicles were forming, causing a lack of development: there is then no base from which antlers can grow. Such a stag is called a hummel; the animal is normal in all other respects, is fertile, and the characteristic is not passed on to the offspring.

Culling for sport or management brings a significant income to the Scottish lowlands and highlands. Nevertheless, an annual cull of about 70,000 red deer has not prevented a population increase of an estimated 360,000 in Great Britain and about 4,000 in Ireland.

SIKA

Sika are an introduced deer species, along with muntjac and the Chinese water deer. (It is true that fallow deer are also not native, but having been with us for over 1,000 years, they are considered more settled than the three Asiatic species.) Our sika are Japanese in origin, introduced to Viscount Powerscourt's estate in Ireland in the mid-nineteenth century. Numerous further introductions (that is, releases) followed, to Bowland Forest in Lancashire, the New Forest, Dorset and Kintyre in western Scotland. Fast forward some 160 years to the 2016 British Deer Society (BDS) survey, and the areas inhabited by sika are broadly around these areas still; only in Scotland have they expanded to the entire western half of the country.

Male sika (stags) stand up to 95cm (37in) at the shoulder, and hinds up to 70cm (28in). Mature examples weigh some 70kg (154lb) and 45kg (100lb), respectively, so they are similar in size to fallow but a little lighter in weight. Back at the larder, dressed but in the skin, a good stag carcass can weigh 45kg (100lb) and a hind around 33kg (72lb).

Sika graze rather than browse, as they have no top incisors but a hard pad, like cattle; they eat heather, grasses, shoots and shrubs, and prefer to lie up in coniferous woodlands. Stags damage trees by gouging the bark, which brings them into conflict with plantation owners and foresters. Sika will also lie up in cereal crops, flattening large areas and so reducing the crop harvest.

It is well recognized that sika are difficult to stalk. Extremely wary deer, they quickly become nocturnal if subjected to much human disturbance. When shot at they can leave an area en masse, not returning for long periods. During culling the advice is to stay hidden after the shot, not to stalk the same areas frequently, and to take deer in more isolated parts first, on the boundary of their main patch, to avoid disturbing recognized resting-up areas.

Identification

Sika have a definite summer and winter coat, varying from a yellow brown or red chestnut in summer with spots, to grey and black in winter, the stags being darker than the hinds. The coat is altogether rougher and thicker than that of the fallow, with stags developing a noticeable mane. There may not be a defined black horseshoe around the bright white rump, which does not run up the back as on a red, but the coat usually has a dark dorsal stripe. There are distinctive white or cream scent glands (metatarsals) on the hocks of the back legs. The head has a 'V' of light hair above the eyes running to the top of the nose, which looks like a furrowed brow. The sika head in relation to its body size is smaller than that of other deer.

A stag has a high-pitched squeal, which then turns into a lower-pitched cry or roar, while a hind will give a high-pitched screech in alarm as a 'heads up' to other deer nearby.

Winter-coated sika hind; note the 'furrowed brow'.

Dark sika stag; note the light hock gland and mane.

Mature stag, hind and calf in summer coat. The black dorsal stripe is just visible on the hind.

Sika stag; note the 45-degree brow tine and the rump patch that does not extend up over the back.

Sika hinds in winter coat. Note the heart-shaped rump, the short tail and the hock glands to the rear legs.

The Sika Year

The rut runs from the end of September to November. Stags can hold a rutting stand, much like fallow, or will occasionally defend a group of hinds from other stags, in the same way as red deer. Stags will groan, blow raspberries, yak yak and whistle during this time. The hinds give birth after a 220-day gestation between May and July; a single calf is born, rarely twins. Weaned by November, sika can breed as yearlings; the young stags will leave areas of dense populations first, settling as much as 30 miles (48km) away. Sika live is small, single-sex groups of no more than six or seven, coming together in greater numbers only for the rut.

The open season for hinds is 1 November to 31 March in England, Wales and Northern Ireland. The close season covers the run-up to birth and while the calf is dependent on its mother; the young are weaned by the beginning of November, which is the opening of the season. Unlike roe, there is no feeling that the season is too long, as sika are seen as an invasive species. Along with other male deer in the UK, the stag season follows sporting considerations: thus the open season is from 1 August to 30 April, the close season being in the summer months to allow the stags to drop and regrow their antlers, and shed their velvet in peace. In Scotland the open season for does is 21 October to 15 February, and 1 July to 20 October for stags.

Antlers

Antlers are cast from April, the oldest animals first, and are fully grown and clean of velvet by August. Sika antlers are similar in structure to the red's but on a smaller scale, with a maximum of eight points. Widely spaced, a feature is the 45-degree angle between the first point and beam, whereas it would be 90 degrees on a red stag. Yearlings usually have a single spike, a brow tine develops in the second or possibly third year, with top points in later years, depending on weather conditions and the quality of food available. The antlers are frequently used to score bark and toss undergrowth, so the tips become white with use.

FALLOW

Fallow are between red and roe deer in size, up to 90cm (35in) for does and 95cm (37in) for bucks at the shoulder. They are similar in height to sika, but a little more heavily built, at up to 56kg (123lb) and 94kg (207lb), respectively. In southern England a good, plump fallow doe will have a larger weight (with the head removed and also the legs at the hocks, and the body cavity empty) of some 38kg (84lb), while a mature buck in fine condition will be up to 59kg (130lb) in the fridge.

Unlike other deer, there are four main types of fallow, differentiated by their coats:

- **Common**, which are tan and fawn with white spots (in summer), becoming more grey and losing some of the spot definition in winter. They have the familiar black horseshoe surrounding the white rump.
- **Menil** are paler than common fallow; they have a light brown horseshoe to the rear, and keep their spots all year.
- **Melanistic** are described as black, but vary from a chocolate to dark grey through to black. Characteristically they have no white coloration at all.

Red and Sika Hybridization

The recently introduced sika is closely related to the red, and will interbreed readily. A worrying problem, zoologists are concerned for the genetic integrity of the indigenous red deer, some saying there are now no more pure reds in mainland Britain. The first generation of a cross has the appearance of both, but descendants following on have the appearance of the dominant parent. This may take the form of a bey tine on a seemingly sika stag (dominant sika, red cross) or a white gland on the back leg of a red, indicating a dominantly red deer but with some sika in its genetic make-up, which makes selective culling impossible. Sika are regarded as pests in some areas and are culled as such. Since 1981 it has been illegal to release sika into the wild (Schedule 9, Wildlife and Countryside Act).

- **White fallow** vary from sandy to white. They are not albino, as they have a normal eye pupil colour.

All fallow except the white show a change of colour tone half way down the body to varying degrees. Fawns do not necessarily follow the mother's colouring; the offspring's coat colour also depends on the sire's colouring, so a herd may well have different coloured members, as the buck will not be present to show lineage.

Of course the antlers and penile sheath are the most obvious differences between the male and female. But from the end of April through to June, bucks cast their antlers, the more mature animals first, prickets later, and in the long grass and growing crops the differences are not then obvious, so it is the thicker neck, the prominent Adams apple and the pedicles on the buck's head that sets them apart. The young male fawn, however, does not start to develop easily visible pedicles until the New Year in its first winter, and is readily mistaken for a doe fawn.

A particular trait of fallow deer is their pronking gait when alarmed. They seem to bounce along with all four feet off the ground at the same time, as opposed to the normal running gait. Does may emit a short bark as a warning to others before moving off in this fashion.

Fallow prefer to inhabit mature woodland with an understorey, but can be found grazing on open grassland and young arable crops, and also on root crops such as carrots, potatoes and parsnips. The harvest in August sees fallow out in the fields, picking over the dropped grain.

Holly, beech mast and shrubs are eaten in the autumn and winter, and bark stripping can be a major problem for landowners at this time. Game-cover crops are a magnet to fallow too, in the same way as maize, resulting in the perennial problem of fallow stunting the growth of these strategically planted smaller strips.

A common and two menil young fallow bucks. The antlers are in velvet, and spots are emerging on the common fallow for the coming summer.

Mature common buck chasing a sore (buck in its 4th year), which is showing signs of palmation.

White fallow buck in velvet; note the eye colour, so it is not albino.

Fallow doe with fawn. Note the fawn's shorter muzzle relative to its head size.

Melanistic fallow buck, sore. The penile sheath hair is very visible, and the long tail. The Adam's apple is prominent even when it is not viewed in profile.

Menil fallow sorrel (buck in its 3rd year).

Fallow are notoriously wary deer, and if stalked continuously will become nocturnal and therefore not shootable under the deer regulations, which state that no deer can be shot earlier than an hour before sunrise or later than an hour after sunset during the respective open seasons.

The Fallow Year

The peak rut takes place in mid-October, but can vary by a few weeks either way. After a gestation of 229 days a single fawn, occasionally twins, is born around June, depending on the date of conception in the rut. Fawns are usually weaned by October, but can feed from the mother into late December.

Bucks and does live apart for most of the year, coming together only for the rut, with young males staying with the does until around eighteen months of age. Does can form very large herds – eighty plus is not unusual – while bucks typically live in smaller groups. Mature bucks are especially secretive for most of the year, but during the rut they become visible on and around their stands, groaning and thrashing to attract does.

The open season in England and Wales for does logically follows this brief description of the yearly cycle, so from 1 November it is permitted to cull them, as fawns are normally independent, and the season closes on 31 March as the does are heavily pregnant by this time. In Scotland because of the harder winter the season is adjusted to run from 21 October to 15 February.

The buck open season is from 1 August right round to 30 April. The three-month close season encompasses the period when the old antlers are dropped and the new ones regrow, so sporting considerations instead rule here. If bucks are shot around or just after the rut, the carcass will often be out of condition, as bucks do not eat much, if at all for that period, expending a lot of energy defending their does from competing bucks. The older bucks, especially, are full of testosterone and not such good eating around this time, some describing the venison as having a metallic taste. Certainly the carcass will have a strong smell, the buck having wallowed in mud and urine as an attractant to does.

Antlers

The male antlers, cast yearly from April, give a reasonable indication of age. They start with a simple spike of 1 to 20cm (½ to 8in) at twelve to twenty-four months old, then a sorrel at three years, a sore at four years showing the start of some palmation, through to a mature buck at five years plus, with fully palmated antlers, having 'spellers' on top with brow and bey (or bez) tines. There is some overlap; perhaps a three-year-old sorrel with a good diet and favourable local conditions can start to palmate, while a sore may show a spindly head if on poor ground. After some eight years, the buck antlers show signs of age, 'going back', indicating the animal is past its prime. Fallow typically live around ten years in the wild and up to sixteen years in captivity.

MUNTJAC

Reeves muntjac are the smallest of the six species found in the UK, and one of the most recently introduced. They are all descended from a number imported from China in 1894 and kept at Woburn Park in Bedfordshire, but deliberate release and escapes from enclosures have led to a feral population. Being well adapted to the UK climate and countryside their numbers have, in recent years, grown exponentially. The BDS 2016 survey shows that muntjac may be found across large areas of England except in the very south-west and south-east, to a northerly limit around Leeds.

Standing just 54cm (21in) at the shoulder and weighing up to 18kg (40lb) live, a mature doe will be around 10kg (22lb) at the larder (with the head off, the legs removed at the hocks, and the body cavity empty), while a buck in the easier conditions of southern England may be up to 13kg (28lb) dressed.

Muntjac are highly adaptable, comfortable in both deciduous and coniferous forests, shrubberies and large gardens – in fact anywhere with a diverse understorey from which they can browse. Unlike larger species they do not cause damage to commercial plantations, but instead can hoover up smaller plants and shrubs when numbers are high, leading to loss of flora diver-

Muntjac buck in winter coat. The V-shaped black lines running up to the pedicles are a distinguishing feature.

Summer-coated muntjac buck; it spends much time lying up ruminating. Note the canine teeth.

Muntjac doe, characterized by a thinner neck and a smaller head with a diamond pattern.

Two muntjac in late March; note the differences between buck and doe.

Muntjac kid: note the spotted back.

sity such as bluebells, primroses, orchids and honeysuckle, which brings them into conflict with gardeners and conservationists. Browse height can be up to a metre if they stand on their hind legs to reach up or push over saplings, from which they eat the lower leaves. Strong for their size, they will push under sturdy fencing to gain access to young plants and shoots on the other side.

Identification

The coat is grey/brown in winter, turning a russet brown in summer. Broadside on, the deer is higher at the haunch than at the shoulder, making its outline appear rather hunched. The face is distinctive, having two sets of glands that are used to mark territories, the most obvious pair (preorbitals) below the eyes. Both male and female have pronounced black facial lines, diamond shaped on a doe, straight lines in a V shape to the pedicles on a buck, which also has long, visible canine teeth. The doe's canines are shorter and do not protrude. These teeth are not ornamental, but are used during fights with other bucks for territory. Scarred necks and chunks missing from ears are not unusual. The antlers are around 10cm (4in) long, with an inward-pointing tip. Mature bucks develop a short brow tine, which is just some 1cm (½in) in length.

The tail of both sexes becomes erect when the deer are alarmed. Muntjac emit a loud bark, repeated at intervals over a long period, both as a warning to other bucks and to attract does. Although bucks are a little larger than does, it is their thick necks, larger heads with canine teeth and of course their antlers that sets them apart from the more slender and elegant-looking does.

The Muntjac Year

Unlike other deer species in the UK, there is no rut period, due to their origin in Asia. There, the year-long warmer climate did not dictate a specific season for birth to maximize survival chances of the young. Instead the muntjac doe can be impregnated almost immediately after giving birth, at any time of the year. A single kid, also widely called a fawn, is born after seven months' (210 days') gestation. A doe can therefore produce three kids every two years; the female kids can themselves become pregnant at seven months, so the muntjac population can rise rapidly. The fawn will have spots along its back, which fade after a few months, and will weigh almost as much as an adult at one year of age.

Bucks shed their antlers in May/June, cleaning their velvet in late August or early September. However, as muntjac buck kids can be born at any time, they could be in velvet any time of the year with their first set of antlers. They do, however, cast these the following spring, then follow the yearly cycle. This is a way of identifying the younger muntjac: in velvet between October and June indicates a kid (fawn).

Counting muntjac in a given area is difficult. They are quite solitary animals; does may be seen with their young, or with a buck, but in no greater numbers. Whereas other species can herd or come out on fields to feed, the muntjac prefers woodland edges or hedgerows at best, never stopping for long in the open, then spending much time lying up ruminating. Since using a thermal imager, I now appreciate just how close you can pass by numerous muntjac, hidden in the undergrowth, unmoving, but intently watching as you pass by.

There is no close season for muntjac as they breed all year. The advice is that if a doe obviously has a dependent fawn, to leave it alone. Taking the more pregnant does means there will not, by this time, be a dependent fawn. Some stalkers do not like to take heavily pregnant does, which is somewhat of a conundrum, as the alternative is perhaps leaving orphaned fawns to die. (*See* Chapter 5 for more on shooting pregnant does.)

All other species of deer in the UK have a close season for bucks, and it seems anomalous that muntjac bucks do not also have a close season during the period they are casting and regrowing their antlers. Perhaps this is because muntjac have only recently become a sporting quarry in their own right. As the stalking scene in the UK matures, perhaps a close season for bucks will emerge. For now, with numbers rapidly rising against a backdrop of new coppices and woodlands being planted countrywide, there appears little appetite for this to happen, as in many areas muntjac are seen as pests and shot on sight.

CHINESE WATER DEER

Chinese water deer (CWD) originate from China and Korea, and were introduced in the late nineteenth century by the Duke of Bedford to Woburn Park alongside muntjac. Releases, both accidental from Whipsnade Zoo (around 1929) and deliberate from other various parks, make for a scattered population across the south-east of England. Bedfordshire, Cambridgeshire, Suffolk and Norfolk hold most of the UK's numbers, estimated at 10 per cent of the world's population of these deer. In their native countries the CWD is on the IUCN 'vulnerable' list because of loss of habitat and poaching. (The International Union for Conservation of Nature is the global authority on the status of the natural world and the measures needed to safeguard it.) The population abroad is said to be declining, but by how much is not reliably ascertainable.

The spread of CWD in England may be curbed by competition for habitat from muntjac, which have adapted very successfully to the UK's flora and climate. Preferring wetlands, the fens of Norfolk provide the ideal habitat, as do reedbeds and river shores, but this species will adapt to drier habitats with a good understorey. Between feeding, these deer will lie up for long periods, ruminating.

The deer are small, just a little taller than muntjac at 50–55cm (20–22in) at the shoulder, lighter in weight, up to 18kg (40lb) live, showing a maximum larder weight of 10kg (22lb) with an empty body cavity, head and legs removed at the hocks. With relatively longer legs than muntjac, they give the appearance of a bigger deer.

CWD feed on grasses, sedge, herbs and woody plants. They do not have top incisor teeth like the sika, so tear rather than cut vegetation. Without antlers, they do not cause damage to trees so do not come into conflict with foresters and landowners, nor conservationists, as the low popula-

CWD spend long periods lying up and ruminating.

tion density is not enough to cause any major loss of local flora.

Identification

The CWD is an even, light brown in summer, and a little darker dull grey in winter, and so they can appear to be like a smaller roe deer. However, there is no lighter-coloured caudal patch, and they have a short tail the same colour as the body. Side on, the rump is noticeably higher than the shoulder. The ears are large in relation to the head, and rounded. Together with black, button-like eyes, they have a teddy bear-like appearance. The bucks do not have antlers, but mature bucks will have noticeable tusks. Does also have tusks, but these are not so prominent. These large canine teeth are somewhat movable, pointing more forward from their resting position when facing up to other bucks.

Both sexes will give a short bark when alarmed, and scream when they are chased. Bucks will whistle and squeak in the run-up to the rut, and 'whicker' when chasing other bucks.

The Chinese Water Deer Year

The rut is in late November and December. Bucks and does form pairs, defending territory from other bucks, staying together until the following April. As with other species, a buck will parallel walk for dominance over a competitor, only fighting if supremacy is not established. Without antlers fatalities are rare, but injuries from tusks are common.

Fawns are born after a six- to seven-month gestation in June or July. Up to three fawns are normal, but six have been recorded. However, a high mortality of some 40 per cent in the first few weeks means the population does not rise rapidly as might initially be assumed. Fawns are

CWD have rounded ears and 'teddy bear' eyes (doe).

CWD buck in its winter coat. It has no rump patch or contrasting tail colour.

CWD buck in its summer coat. Note that the rump is higher than the shoulders.

CWD buck skull. Tusks are the dominant feature in these specimens.

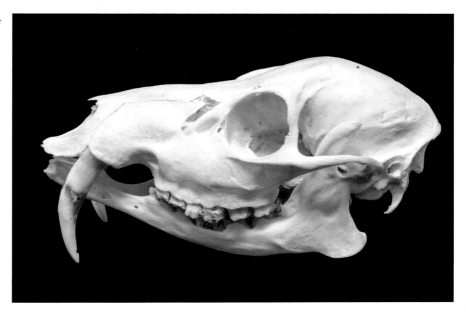

hidden in cover, for the first few days emerging only to suckle.

At other times, CWD live a more solitary life, excepting does with fawns, which form small groups only on a good feeding area.

OPEN SEASON

Interestingly, the open season for both male and female is 1 November to 31 March in England (the species not being found in Scotland, Wales or Northern Ireland). This is understandable for the doe, as she may well have dependent fawns before November. The buck, having no antlers, does not have the cachet of other species as a sporting quarry, although the tusks in a mounted head are of interest. As the sexes are so similar in appearance, the same close season for bucks has been applied, in order to protect does in the latter stages of pregnancy and with fawns at foot. Numbers are not great, and animals have died out in other areas where they have been introduced, so perhaps a close season is to the good. Certainly CWD are a minor species in the UK sporting and conservation scene, since they do not cause significant damage nor are they expanding greatly in number.

Chapter 4

Deer Sight, Hearing and Olfactory Capabilities

There has been much discussion by hunters about exactly how much deer can see and hear us. This matters hugely, as it informs how we should dress, approach and act when deer are nearby, so as not to alarm them. A large industry has developed from this often flawed understanding, including the sale of hunter camouflage clothing, both scent blockers and attractants, imitative calls, and licks of various flavours. Rather than discuss my own and other stalkers' experiences exclusively, which may be specific to our own environments and often depends on a personal gauge of noise and so on, I sought the input of research scientist Dr George Gallagher, Dana Professor of Animal Science at Berry College in Georgia, USA, who specializes in these areas. His experience is with the American whitetail deer, but it is widely accepted that different species of deer share the same traits and capabilities. There is no reason why Professor Gallagher's findings do not apply to our six species here in the UK, and I have summarized them at the end of the chapter in order to demonstrate the implications for deer stalkers.

EYESIGHT

Professor Gallagher and his department research deer from a viewpoint that is different from a hunter's. He studies the anatomy and physiology of the various parts first, as this dictates the behaviour of the animals; thus with eyesight, deer act in a certain way because they see that way.

As we know, all mammal eyesight is broadly similar, each creature having two eyes (binocular vision), enabling distance perception through the brain, which compares the images obtained from each eye. A lens at the front of each eye focuses light entering through the pupil, the opening surrounded by a variable iris, which closes or opens according to the level of ambient light.

Human view (left) and the deer view (right). Note the muted colours perceived, and the reduced acuity or clarity of deer sight.

In bright conditions the pupil contracts to allow less light in, while at night the pupil dilates, gathering more ambient light. In simple terms, light is focused on the rear of the eye, the retina, where sensitive receptors capture the image as colour and movement; these signals are sent to the brain, which interprets them as sight. The similarity between human and deer eyesight ends when we start to compare the capabilities of each part.

The Differences between the Eyes of Deer and Humans

Looking firstly at the lens, the human eye has the ability to change its shape: this is called accommodation. This allows us to focus close up, at something held in our hands perhaps, or at a greater distance, across a field or at the top of a hill far away.

The lens in a deer's eye, and in many other animals, is almost fixed and has little ability to change. Vision in deer seems to be adjusted for best perception at relatively close quarters, equating to what we would call nearsightedness; in deer this is dictated by the shape of the eye, not the lens, as in human nearsightedness. If we then look at the back of the eye, the human retina has a range of rod receptors and three types of cone receptors. These cones contain photopigments, giving colour to sight, and are receptive to short, moderate and longer wavelengths of light in turn, roughly equating to blue, green and red: for us, this is our full rainbow of colours, called trichromatic colour vision. The rod receptors are sensitive to low light levels, but not colour, which gives us monochromatic vision in near darkness: human cones need something more than bright moonlight to produce colour vision.

The deer retina is vastly different. Deer have many more rod receptors than we do, enabling much better sight in near darkness. Rods are also more sensitive to movement than cones, which is another advantage that deer have across their large field of view. They have just two types of cone receptor, enabling sight of short and moderate wavelengths in colour only. It is likely that this allows deer to see blue intensely, earth tones and yellow, while greens and reds are probably seen as grey tones.

There are two further differences between deer and human eyes. Deer have a tapetum, a layer that effectively reflects light received by the eye back over the receptors of the retina a second time, which further enhances low light vision. This is seen when shining a light at deer in the dark, when the light seems to come straight back at you. The combined effect of having many more

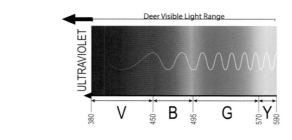

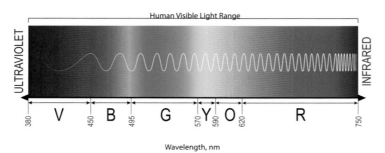

Difference between deer and human colour vision.

Deer have no UV filter in their eyes as humans do, so their eyesight probably extends into the ultraviolet

The colour spectrum seen by the human eye as compared to that seen by a deer.

This deer, caught by flash, shows the reflective tapetum clearly in the eyes.

rod receptors and the tapetum means that deer have much better sight and movement detection than humans in low light conditions.

Deer do not have the UV filter we have in our eyes, which probably enables their vision to dip into the ultraviolet range, beyond what we see as blue, the limit of our spectrum of vision. This has implications for clothed human detection.

Not only are the number and type of receptors important, but also their distribution across the retina. Humans have more cones, but they are concentrated in the centre of the retina. Deer have far fewer cones, but they are spread across the retina on a horizontal plane, giving greater peripheral vision. This is complemented by the pupil, which is round in the human eye but resembles a horizontal slit in deer. Thinking of cones in the context of pixels in a digital camera, the more pixels there are, the higher the resolution. So humans have a wider colour spectrum and greater clarity of image compared to deer, but in a small central area.

Deer sight excels in having a wide field of view, but with an almost fixed focus. Everything is in focus equally to a mid-distance, at a lower resolution. Our eyes are positioned relatively close together, enabling us to concentrate on fixed points, such as this needle and thread in our fingers or that rabbit 75m away; this is ideal for us as a predator species, with around a 170-degree field of view. In contrast the deer has eyes on each side of its head, making for 310-degree vision. This makes it possible, for example, for deer to run through thick cover without crashing into trees and branches; human sight is more directional, and we need to look at obstacles actively and focus on each one to avoid them, which slows us down in such an environment.

For Professor Gallagher, the way the deer eye has evolved explains why they are crepuscular (active at twilight): their vision is skewed towards the colour blue, which is the spectrum of light most available at dusk and dawn. Together with enhanced low-light vision, nearsightedness, and the ability to detect movement across a wide field of view, these are all traits we associate with a species that is wary of predators. The eyes had to be that way for deer to behave in that way.

The pupil in deer resembles a horizontal slit, as opposed to the circular human pupil.

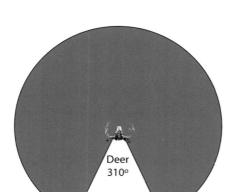 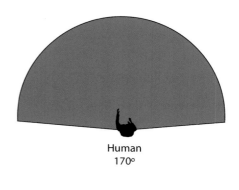

A deer's field of view compared to a human's.

DEER HEARING

Professor Gallagher calls deer hearing and the sense of smell tough areas of research. This is partly due to habituation – the possibility that deer may not respond to a sound or smell because they have become used to it over time. As it does not register as a danger, so it does not elicit a response we can observe. Given this, how can we know if deer hear certain noises or just choose to ignore them? There are a number of examples to show this could be the case. First, take gas guns, used to scare birds from planted seed crops just beginning to show through. Many of us have seen deer in the vicinity of these, ignoring the regular loud bangs. But let off a rifle, broadly similar to a gas gun – although it is possible to tell them apart – and deer disappear immediately.

Then there are farm tractors going about their daily business, again mainly ignored by deer. I've sat in a high seat while crops have been sprayed early in the spring, also while being cut in August, and have seen at first hand deer coming out to feed on nearby rides, seemingly oblivious to the disturbance. But approach a field with deer out in the open in your truck and they invariably move off. Riders on horseback are also largely ignored by deer, which seem to be aware that these intruders on their space do not pose a danger, again something they have learned through habituation.

DEER SENSE OF SMELL

With smell, the olfactory sense, deer can appear to ignore what to our noses are seemingly strong smells. When I started stalking back in the 1980s, I had numerous outings with a professional who would light a roll-up cigarette during each stalk. Tobacco smoke has a distinctive smell, especially in the context of a wood, being alien to the environment. Of course I don't know if we would have seen more deer if he hadn't lit up, but we were never short of deer to see or shoot. Perhaps the deer didn't register tobacco as associated with human danger, but also there is no way to know for sure that they actually sensed the smoke at all. It could be that, being a 'foreign' smell, it just wasn't on their nasal radar, so to speak. Perhaps one could argue that the alien tobacco smoke masked the more recognizable human smells and aided our stalking forays, but the point is that it cannot be proven either way.

TESTING DEER FOR RESPONSES

Laboratory procedures are available that could possibly be modified in an attempt to count the number of specialized olfactory nerve cells found on the tubinate bones of the sinus cavity, which would likely be an expensive proposition. Claims on the internet of deer having 20, 100 and 500

Although the sika on the right appears to be focusing on the camera, the deer on the left is just as aware.

times the sensitivity of humans can easily be found, but might not answer the questions asked. We may assume more olfactory receptors means a more acute sense of smell, but it may just be different, in a similar way that human and deer vision differs.

Given the possibilities of a lack of response to different stimuli, research into deer senses has concentrated on hearing in the States, using sedated deer to bypass sensed but ignored stimuli, called auditory brainstem response tests.[1] Briefly the deer, having had electrodes placed at three points on the skull, had external noise at various frequencies and intensities played to them. The electrical responses by the brain picked up by the electrodes demonstrated that deer heard sounds within a certain frequency band. The experiments were carried out to ascertain the hearing range of white-tailed deer, but the results throw

up interesting information for us in the UK. These are summarized as follows:

Deer showed a response to sounds from 0.25kHz to 30kHz; the best sensitivity was found to be between 4kHz and 8Khz. Other researchers, again in the States, experimenting on bighorn sheep and desert mule deer had found broadly similar results. This should not be surprising, as deer vocalizations have shown to be in the range of 3kHz to 6.5kHz. There is no value in being attuned to sounds outside those made by other members of the same species, and predators will not make noises when approaching, so there is nothing useful from that angle, either. However, danger or warnings can be transmitted between deer when spotted visually by sound. Stalkers are familiar with the low moans and grunts made by bucks during the rut; these are the sounds that carry furthest, attracting does from afar. Meanwhile the high frequency squeaks made by fawns to their mothers don't carry a long way, minimizing the chance of attracting predators. As these overlap somewhat with the range of frequencies that humans hear best – 2kHz to 5kHz – the bottom line is that deer do not make sounds that we cannot hear.

As for the sound levels required to elicit a response during the tests, these ranged from around 65db (which is the equivalent of unstrained conversation at 3–5ft/1–1.5m) at the lowest and highest frequencies, down to around 40db (library background noise) at 4 to 8kHz. This isn't brilliant hearing, but the researchers were looking to gain a response via electrodes placed around the head. It should be noted, however, that behavioural testing may be more sensitive at determining minimum hearing thresholds than auditory brainstem response tests.

Perhaps deer are a little more sensitive to sounds than laboratory tests suggest, but if these results show that deer may not have fantastic hearing, where do they get the reputation of having great sensory capabilities? It must be noted that the deer's outer ears (the pinnae) are much larger than ours, and can move independently of each other to focus on certain sounds. These two factors alone make for more precise hearing.

But we also need to remember that the woods and fields are their home. They live there 24/7, and it is usually a quiet place. The background noises of birds and wind in the trees are everyday normality, as are the intermittent noises of squirrels and other small mammals looking for food and chasing each other around. The experienced stalker knows that when he arrives at a high seat, it will take a good twenty to thirty minutes before the woods come alive again, his presence having at first induced a hush. The hunter's footsteps and the noise he makes brushing past brambles and ferns, then climbing the steps are telegraphed by all animals and birds in the wood. Deer are aware of this, hence it is common for a stalker on foot to miss a good number of deer in a wood. They simply slip away well before it is possible to see them, alerted in advance.

Understanding this demonstrates why deer hearing doesn't need to be fabulously good. It's the deer's awareness of its environment that keeps it from danger. If deer do then pick up on a certain sound, or perhaps birds flying off en masse, those large ears rotate to concentrate on a specific area and gather more information from that direction.

SUMMARY

Sight is probably the most misunderstood of the senses, as it is difficult to imagine vision that is different to our own. The image at the beginning of the chapter shows what deer can most likely see, but it is the detection of movement that is the most important feature of the animal's visual sense. This is why the stationary hunter is less detectable to deer. One can demonstrate this in the field by moving directly towards a deer. As long as the person is not bobbing and weaving, the deer will not easily sense the approaching hunter, which is seen as a still object. But move sideways by one or two steps and the animal immediately detects the movement and takes flight. Experienced hunters know to stalk directly towards a deer in plain sight.

Given that movement detection is of paramount importance to deer, it is not at all certain that camouflage apparel will hide a hunter's movements any better than plain clothing would. Anecdotally, the stalkers whom I have been with in the woods who were wearing camouflage don't seem to have any better success, or get any closer to deer than I do in plain greens and browns. Advertisements extolling the effectiveness of branded camouflage patterns usually have an image of a hunter blending into the surrounding woodland. This looks effective, but it misses the point, for as soon as the hunter moves, perhaps to raise their rifle or to move forwards, the advantage is lost.

Scent is important, too. Of course we need to stalk into the wind to avoid our scent being ahead of us, but further than that we should also strive to reduce our own scent overall, so as to avoid it being spread around our immediate vicinity by eddies of swirling wind. Washing our clothing in unperfumed detergent and softener is not difficult nowadays, and the same goes for personal shower gel, shampoo and deodorant. Possibly, following the discussion above, it could be that deer do not register the various perfumes in most household products anyway. They may, or they may not – but why risk it? For years I have washed my stalking clothing and myself in scent-free products because I think it makes a difference, and I feel I'm doing my best to minimize my human odour footprint while in the woods; it doesn't take a huge effort to do this. Many of these unperfumed products do not have UV brighteners either, normally added to most modern 'biological' detergents to make coloured clothing look more vibrant. For deer, the fact that they can probably see into the UV range will make clothing washed in such detergents stand out brightly against foliage. And if a camouflage pattern has been printed on the material, it will not be able to hide the wearer to any extent, even if he doesn't move.

The discussion of deer hearing and noise should not surprise anyone who has spent time in the countryside. We need to keep noise to a minimum, and be aware that animals take cues from each other. Wood pigeons flying off in a flock above us, and pheasants alarmed from underfoot, are an immediate giveaway and will alert deer – but there are other, more subtle indicators, too. This is why stalking in pairs or in a group can work extremely well if done occasionally. Deer quietly moving away from a human presence can be ambushed by a stationary stalker, perhaps sat in a high seat, as long as the deer are not alarmed to the point of running, when shots are then not possible. When targeting the more wary species of fallow and sika, such co-ordinated stalks will yield better results than stalking alone.

Chapter 5

Deer Stalking

THE DEER-STALKING LANDSCAPE

The deer-stalking landscape has changed very much in the last fifteen years. Interest in the practice has increased dramatically, whether as recreation, or through necessity as part of a cull programme. Unfortunately this has had a monetary effect, and deer stalking is now big business.

Obtaining Ground

There are fewer casual permissions available now for the stalker looking for land. Farmers and landowners are running businesses, and another reliable source of income for which they don't have to put much time into is highly appealing. On the other side of this is the would-be stalker, willing to pay for a tract of land to stalk over, so a 'supply and demand' situation exists. But demand has outstripped supply and, as happens in any other commercial area, the price of leases has risen accordingly, most often going to the highest bidder. It's not unheard of for a resident stalker with a lease due to be renewed to find him- or herself gazumped, a syndicate taking over the stalking alongside their other leases.

The novice shouldn't be disheartened, however. There is land available on the basis of a handshake, where the landowner is more interested in the person holding the rifle and doing an honest job for him or her than in money – but getting into that position of trust is the hard part. Why should a landowner entertain a knock on the door and let an unknown person loose on his or her land with a gun?

A lot of forethought and planning needs to go into such an approach. Rabbit, rat, squirrel and crow shooting around an estate can be a way in, as is beating for the local shoot, but it may take some years to gain someone's confidence such that one is allowed to deer stalk. Becoming an assistant to an ageing stalker can work for both parties. It is a great help to a stalker in their sixties or seventies to have some young blood drag heavy carcasses in return for some shots, as long as the assistant knows their place. Many a stalker has been drawn to the sport or occupation in the first place precisely because they like to operate alone and don't want a chatty helper!

Leases and Monetary Returns

However land is acquired, one should not accept a third party's estimate of deer in a given area. A paid lease that seemed inexpensive may turn out to be the opposite if far fewer deer were actually there than expected. Past stalking records can be helpful, unless the last leaseholder shot nearly everything available, leaving nothing for the new tenant until it naturally restocked after some years. Much also depends on the aim of a lease.

The stubble is all ploughed in by early August; only the game-cover crop is a draw for fallow.

Not disturbing horses and local residents overrides the desire to cull just a few deer.

may call for a lot of time to be spent in high seats overlooking the saplings or game cover, which grows out of kilter with usual arable crops as it is planted in late summer to mature around November to hold game birds.

One of my permissions is owned by a delightful couple who like to see deer on their land when they take their dogs for a walk. The farm manager, however, can see the loss caused by too many deer, so we have come to a compromise in stalking just one day a month. My job is to 'take the top off them', and remove all evidence of my having being there. Occasionally over the years I've had a call to say they are happy with the deer population as it presently is and to leave be for the next season. I would like to do more, but it is their land and they can do what they wish with it. I'm just happy to be their stalker of choice, as it's in a beautiful part of the country!

The landowner could want just a few deer taken, and the proceeds split so that he or she ends up with some fillets in their freezer. Another scenario could be that a new tree plantation or game cover is being decimated, meaning that many fallow need to be shot intensively. This

Large commercial softwood plantations often require contractors to cull deer at night.

I've also been called to areas with 'too many deer', only to record just three or four roe on a trail 'cam' occasionally jumping a fence and feeding on a grassy field. One such area I surveyed was close to horse paddocks and houses, so I declined. I dont see that stalking should entail the eradication of small pockets of deer, in the course of which other animals and humans are unnecessarily disturbed. Deer are part of our flora and fauna, and it is a matter of balancing the needs of the interested parties; a few resident deer are not going to make a huge difference, in fact they enhance an area with their presence.

Commercial Culling

Commercial shooting of deer is another issue altogether, for which contractors are employed. Large tracts of land are planted with softwoods such as spruce and are grown as a crop, as a long-term investment. Deer are seen as pests in these areas, and licences are granted for night shooting with appropriate equipment. This is not sport, but a strategy to protect business interests.

One can see that there are all sorts of possibilities, and a lease isn't a green light to do whatever the holder wishes. If the stalker doesn't fulfil the requirements, he or she will have their contract terminated. One needs to spend time assessing the ground, finding whether deer are resident or more transient, perhaps lying up in a large nearby wood, but venturing on to the prospective tract of land at night. If this is the case, questions arise as to whether the land can be stalked to the satisfaction of the landowner. Much damage to trees and young crops can be inflicted by a herd of deer at night, and the stalker is almost powerless to stop this. His or her only recourse will be to ambush the herd on their way to or from the fields at dawn or dusk. Deer will, however, quickly become wise to this, and if unduly harassed may either move away from the area altogether, or feed only during the hours of darkness, leading to the land being virtually unstalkable.

I experienced this on one estate of mostly arable land, but was able to take many of the offending fallow from the holding wood that belonged to another family. The situation was explained to the satisfaction of the owner of

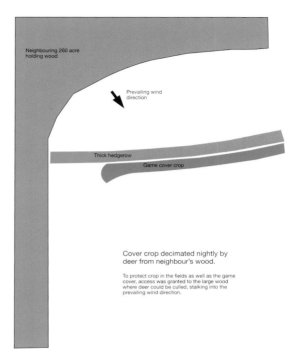

Neighbouring woods hold deer during the day.

the fields, for they had relatively few carcasses at the end of the year despite many shots heard. However, the arable land was vital in controlling the fallow, as it allowed access to the holding wood, being downwind of the prevailing weather.

Before taking any permission, it goes without saying that the stalker needs to walk the perimeter of the land, noting all the footpaths, bridleways and shortcuts used by the public when dog walking. He or she will then have a reasonable understanding of the area and its topography, knowing where shots are possible and where they are not. The estate manager and farm workers can be great sources of information, too, sharing favoured deer locations and the times of the day they are seen.

Seeking deer runs and favoured routes between woods and coppices is never wasted effort. The best time of year for this is around March, when the woods have lost the fern undergrowth over winter, making deer paths and

Fallow had the run of this area over winter, the effects of which are very visible in March.

scrapes easily visible. Deer themselves are also moving around, searching for food, often on the new crop showing through in the open. Forays at night with a thermal device can help enormously with a deer survey, as you will never see all the deer in a given area during the day.

Moving deer past a spotter can work in some circumstances, too. We once pushed through a 4-acre (1.6ha) fenced plantation of young trees that had become overgrown with ferns and bramble, expecting to move some four or five muntjac, judging from the one or two burrows under the surrounding stout 2m fence. But we were surprised to count thirteen muntjac and six roe emerging from the opened gate.

From these sorts of activities one can get a sense of the deer population and the likely cull achievable. If it concurs with the landowner's estimates, a lease can be discussed. I am loath to give any price guideline, as so many variables need to be taken into account. But the part-time stalker should be aware from the outset that there is no profit to be made from a few fairly

small permissions. He or she has to account for the cost of stalking equipment, a vehicle, chiller, insurance and his or her time – and that's not including the cost of a lease! At best, stalking should be seen as a highly enjoyable but relatively expensive and time-consuming recreation, which will return some carcass money to cover fuel, cartridges and a little clothing.

Cull Plans

With a lease or permission sorted, the stalker will need to assess what can be taken from the ground. There are all manner of stalking cull plans that can be followed based on census data, such as dung counting and cohort analysis, some of which are quite scientific in approach. Perhaps the most quoted is the simple maintenance cull, which will keep the population stable. It involves culling the birthrate by taking a third of all young, juvenile, mature and older animals from a population containing more females than males per year. Using this method, more than half of the deer culled should be female.

If a reduction in the deer population is required, it simply may be that as many female deer as possible are culled until the population shows a noticeable decline, then a maintenance cull can be implemented. A more balanced cull will then consider the male-to-female ratios, 1:1 being the aim, although this is rarely achieved. This may seem like a 'blunt instrument' approach, but consider that in the patchwork of land ownership across southern England, deer will travel across many borders. What were 'your' deer yesterday are the next door neighbour's but one today, and maybe for the next two weeks, unless they decide to move on – or back to your permission. How can the hunter formulate a coherent plan in the light of this?

The answer, for many of us, is that we cannot. We have to take our cue from the landowner, who will decide if the number of deer on his or her land is unacceptable, having obtained advice from the farm manager, the forester who plants their trees, and of course the stalker.

On one small permission I have, the initial cull was based around the decimation of a large wildflower garden. After some years of culling muntjac on sight, I now take a couple of these small

Sika herd on neighbouring land.

deer a year, as there is no more mass destruction of wild flowers. This is a simple case of first, identifying the aim; second, reducing the deer accordingly; followed by third, population maintenance at an acceptable level.

TAKING TO THE FIELD

Having discussed obtaining a firearms licence and the law (Chapter 1), equipment (Chapter 2), deer species and how they perceive us (Chapters 3 and 4), ground to shoot over and thoughts on cull planning (above), it's time to take to the field and discuss shot placement. This subject seems to take up as many column inches in the press and online as do calibre discussions. Two areas dominate, starting with the ethics of head and neck shooting, with the inherent risk of wounding with a slight misplacement of the shot. This is contrasted with heart/lung shots and the loss of edible meat through bone splinters, bruising and blood seepage into muscle tissue, discussed in Chapter 2, bullet choice, and at the end of this chapter. The second and perhaps largest area

discusses shooting distance: how far is too far for an ethical shot? While these interlinked points are endlessly debatable, there are some factors to consider that all stalkers can agree on. For myself, a defendable framework can be established from these criteria.

Size of the Target

First, a heart/lung shot encompasses a good 15cm (6in) circle within which the shooter can aim on roe; this is a little larger for fallow, sika and red at, say, 20cm (8in), and smaller for muntjac and Chinese water deer, at about 10cm (4in). Outside of this area, the shot may not be immediately fatal. Meanwhile, a head and neck shot has perhaps a 5cm (2in) circle in which to aim. When these shots are discussed, in reality the brain and spine are targeted, so anywhere in front of the eyes is not going to kill a deer side on. The 1cm (½in) diameter spinal cord is encased in the spinal bones, together a long, curved, tubular target the diameter of a toilet-roll holder. Clip the spine with a bullet and the deer may not collapse: one needs to rely on a bullet fragmenting to catch the spinal cord or to cause much damage locally to disrupt the cord.

Now consider the rifle, and the man or woman holding it. A reasonably good rifle will shoot a 1in group at 100yd from a good stable rest: that is, 1 'minute of angle', or MOA (actually 1.047in, to be precise) (*see* box). This easily doubles to 2in (2 MOA) in the field for numerous reasons, including shooting from a less than stable support, cold hands and body, awkward shooting angle, poor light, a cross-wind, buck fever, or a combination of all these factors. Taking the 6in roe target, this could be hit at 300yd, given the right elevation adjustment for a falling bullet (2 MOA at 300yd = 6in, *see* box); however, this needs to be practised and verified on paper prior to shooting at live animals.

A 2in circle for head and neck shots given 2 MOA limits the shot to 100yd. Plenty of stalkers have a rifle capable of ½in groups at 100yd, at the range, perhaps lying down in the stable prone position or sitting at a stout table, the front and rear of the rifle supported, shooting a known distance. It's different in the field, however, and these examples, I believe, are 'real world' figures.

So for me, 300yd (274m) for a heart/lung shot is the maximum distance I could shoot roe, given ideal conditions. It would be a good deal less for smaller deer, but not more for larger deer. This means I would not attempt a shot at a roe at 300yd with a strong crosswind in the rain when I was cold and wet, from a pair of crossed sticks. But I might consider doing so on a calm day, lying down with the rifle on a bipod, if I couldn't get closer.

I'll spine or brain shoot deer to about 80yd, given the following conditions:

- **The animal is unaware of my presence.** This ensures the head isn't constantly bobbing up and down, or that the deer will not suddenly run just as the trigger is pulled. I've brain shot many a feeding or resting deer, ruminating: it's a very humane and legitimate target.
- **I have a good and stable rest.** In recent years I've used four-leg sticks exclusively, such that I am comfortable with shooting head or necks at 80yd (c.70m), or a heart shot to around 200yd (180m) on fallow. I find the sticks are reliably steady, even when looking through the scope for a period of time waiting for an animal to turn into a good, shootable position. I'll shoot somewhat further with a bipod and rear support, although I rarely do.
- **I have a safe backstop.** On level ground, a head or neck shot may not always be possible, and a body shot is then the only option.

When targeting the head, it is safer to shoot front or rear on, because a low shot (if central) will then hit the spine. A slight misplacement of a side-on shot can end up in the jaw, or lower down, taking out the oesophagus, and a long and unpleasant death can then result if a second shot cannot be taken.

In sum, various external factors come together to inform the hunter about his or her proposed shot. I use the 300yd (274m) body

---

Minute of Angle (MOA) Explained

Imagine a rifle is at the centre of a 100yd radius circle, shooting outwards. If the rifle can put three bullets a combined 1in apart on a target at the edge, 100yd away, the angular spread is 1 'minute of angle', or 'MOA' (1/60th of a degree). This minute measurement is dependent on distance, so at 50yd it will be 1/2in, at 200yd 2in, and at 400yd 4in. At 1,000yd, 1 MOA is 10in; 2 MOA is 2 minutes of angle, so at 200yd would be 4in. As distance increases, the spread increases, but the angle remains the same. This is convenient for the rifleman, who can describe how accurate his rifle is in these terms. A really accurate target rifle may shoot 1/4 MOA, which would put the three bullets no more than 1/4in apart at 100yd, and 1in apart at 400yd, all things being equal.

Another way to work out angular spread at distance uses Milradians, which translate more easily to metric measurements and scope adjustment. I use MOA here just as an example to demonstrate a point about shooting at distance.

shots and 80yd (c.70m) head/neck shots as a working maximum, and any other factors will reduce that distance.

Professional stalkers who shoot upwards of 250 deer in a year may have a different take on these distances, but for the recreational stalker who shoots only ten or fifteen deer a year it is a different matter, as he or she will not have sufficient familiarity with bullet drop, wind and equipment, nor have had the necessary practice to perform longer shots reliably.

The Importance of Collapsing Blood Pressure

At any distance over 80m (90yd) I take a high heart shot – that is, one-third up the body in line with the back of the front leg. Some advocate a little lower to catch the heart full on, but the top of the heart is where the major blood vessels come into it (the superior vena cava and the pulmonary vein) and also lead from it (the aorta,

and the pulmonary artery). Destroying these will cause an immediate collapse of blood pressure, meaning the deer will more than likely drop and die within a few metres. A shot that destroys just the heart muscle itself will certainly cause death, but there are valves between the ventricles and the blood vessels that will maintain the blood pressure in the body for a little longer, which means the deer may run quite some distance before expiring. No doubt it is clinically dead at the shot, but potentially it will be hard to find.

There is another area to target that has some following, called the Hilar shot. It aims to put the bullet at the junction of the trachea with the left and right bronchus at the forward part of the lungs. This area is rich in blood vessels, and a strike here will quickly disable the animal, causing its near instant collapse. Its aim point is some 8cm (3in) forwards of the high heart shot, vertically level with the front of the foreleg. Some report much meat damage to the shoulders if a little wayward, but I have little experience with this shot and stick to what works for me.

Shots that strike outside these zones are likely not to cause near instant death, but will be fatal

High heart shot exit wound and resultant viscera, showing a good kill with little meat damage. Compare this to the next image. The deer was dropped on the spot (6.5×55, Swift Scirocco).

Schematic of the vital organs. The heart and major blood vessels are in red, the lungs in orange, the brain purple and the neck vertebrae in yellow. The liver (blue) is further back, lying against the diaphragm, which separates it from the lungs. It is not a target organ.

Aim areas for different shots. The oblique heart shot is found by aiming between the front legs, approximately one third up the body.

Aim points obliquely from the front. Between the front legs, one third up the body has the greatest margin of allowable error compared to the neck or head shot.

Neck shot not on, and an unsafe back stop. A high heart shot aim point is shown.

nonetheless. A search may well be necessary to locate the carcass, as in the heart shot, above.

Lung Shots

A lung shot, about midway up a broadside deer in line with the front leg is effective, but bullet choice is key. Remembering the lungs are kept expanded in the thoracic cavity by a vacuum, a very frangible bullet may cause a large entry wound and enter a little way inside the body, collapsing one lung. The other lung will still be viable, so the deer runs off, no doubt to shortly die, but a long track may be necessary.

Better is a bullet that expands reliably and passes through both lungs and exits. With a decent hole in both sides of the ribcage, both lungs collapse, causing rapid death. Blood at the scene will be bright red and frothy, having been just oxygenated in the lungs.

Forward of a heart/lung shot is a shoulder shot. With a suitably powerful round and again a controlled expanding bullet, both shoulders will be broken if the deer is broadside on. The deer will not move far and by disrupting the major blood vessels in between, a good kill should result. There may be a large amount of meat loss with this shot however, which is why many advocate instead a high heart shot, all things being equal. Shoulder shots are often promoted in Africa

A frontal neck shot can carry on and re-enter the body, causing extensive meat damage.

where you want to anchor your animal in large expanses of open land and meat loss isn't so much of a concern.

A high shot placement above the shoulders or lungs can result in a spine shot. The animal will be down immediately without moving off, but not dead. After such a shot, the stalker needs to ensure the deer is dispatched quickly with (preferably) another shot, or with a knife inserted at the jugular furrow at the base of the neck, the knife being directed back towards the entrance of the chest to sever the major blood vessels – the aorta running to the head, for example. This is not advisable when dealing with a large buck or a deer not hugely disabled at the front end by the shot, as a flailing head may be dangerous to the stalker with knife in hand. A close-range shot is best in this case.

WAYWARD SHOTS

After some experience, a hunter may instinctively know if he or she has taken a bad shot; it will surely happen at some point in their stalking career. There will not be a distinctive thwack of the bullet strike, or the animal will move in an unexpected way immediately after the shot. Here the hunter needs to pause and assess. A search with binoculars or a thermal imager should be the next move. If nothing is found visually, the hunter should range the shot, if he or she has not already done so.

Marking the spot where the shot was taken, and scraping a line or pointing a branch towards the shot direction for future reference if needed, the hunter will make their way towards the strike area. When reached, he or she should look back and range to where the shot was taken, confirming he is in the correct spot. Only then should a search begin, for it is easy to become disoriented on the way to a strike area over undulating ground, and start the search short of or further away from where the bullet actually struck. Blood, pins (hair) and bone are the main signs to spot, but there is more.

A mortally wounded deer tends to run *through* undergrowth, not past or around it. Unusually bent ferns or hair on bramble indicating that a single deer passed straight by can give a clue to the direction, as can scraped hoofprints in mud. The deer may not be able to run on all four legs, and may be dragging a leg. If the hunter spots blood, he or she then marks the spot and moves on.

Once the stalker gets a definite direction, they may be able to predict the next blood splash and move a little faster towards the carcass, but sometimes a blood trail will stop. It could be that as a deer breathes in while running, blood will stop leaking from the wound site, but will start again some metres on. Once the deer is found, one needs to ensure the animal is dead before approaching of course, so look for chest or head movement. If none, approach from its rear and touch an eye with sticks to make sure there is no reaction.

If the animal is still alive, a follow-up shot is the best way to finish the job. At close quarters, the hunter needs to remember to aim high, as the scope crosshairs are typically some 1.5in (3.8cm) above the path of the bullet. Many a 3m shot has been missed by forgetting this in the heat of the moment!

Liver and Gut Shots

A shot further back from the heart will encounter the liver or, further back still, the stomach (rumen). The liver-shot deer will hunch and move off without much, if any, blood being lost. What blood is found will be dark red. With a good expanding bullet the liver will be badly damaged and the animal will bleed out internally nearby, as the liver not only stores some 10 per cent of the body's blood volume, but also has a lot of blood passing through it from the portal vein and hepatic artery. Without a blood trail such a shot deer may need careful tracking if it moves far.

The gut-shot deer will also hunch up and run off stiff-legged. Gut content and light-coloured belly hair more than blood may be at the site, and presents a problem in that it is not fatal for quite some time. Each scenario is different, but generally the stalker would not look for this animal straightaway. Left to rest up for a few hours or overnight if shot at last light, the deer may have stiffened and may not want to rise and move off when found, thus presenting the chance of another shot when quietly approached.

Broken Limbs

Misplaced shots do happen, and broken legs can result from a low strike. Just a little blood and some bone splinters may be at the site. Often such a shot deer will run off, covering the first 20m or so full of adrenalin, such that the broken limb may not be noticeable to the stalker. Thereafter the gait will indicate a problem, if the deer is still in sight. This sort of wounded deer may be the hardest to find; the animal can travel a long way as the injury isn't life threatening, and maybe over a boundary where the stalker has no permission to be. Again, leaving well alone and a careful approach with the possible boundary to your back much later on may be the best method, perhaps without a dog unless steady at heel. The deer may stand when encountered but be loath to move off. The stalker must be ready for a quick but safe shot, or the moment will be lost.

Such a low strike, being way off target, needs some careful thought as to why it happened. Perhaps a branch deflected the bullet, but at the very least the rifle should be fired at a target to see if is still shooting to point of aim before a live animal is stalked again.

Quartering Shots

If not broadside on, the stalker needs to know the internal arrangement of the organs to best place a bullet. A deer facing 10 o'clock away from the rifle needs to be precisely shot, if no other opportunity is likely to present itself (*see* page 74). A bullet tucked in by the first rib will pierce the diaphragm, taking out a lung and/or top of the heart, exiting in front of the opposite shoulder. Enough damage will have been caused for a good kill, assuming the bullet stays together but mushrooms nicely.

The quartering on deer should be taken with a shot that enters just in front of the shoulder, to traverse the thoracic cavity and out behind the opposite shoulder (page 74). In effect the bullet path is the reverse of the deer that is facing at 10 o'clock away.

The frontal chest shot can cause huge meat damage. A friend with a .243 has shot a number of fallow this way to good effect, the bullet stopping before encountering the saddle or haunches. I favour a heavier calibre and bullet weight, so in this (rare) scenario I will wait for the deer to turn, or I'll choose to pass up the shot. A 165g .308 bullet will easily pass the whole length of a sika, exiting or coming to rest against the femur in a haunch. Of course the deer will be dead, but there will be massive meat damage and gut content released internally, too, and the stalker could well be looking at a carcass entirely unfit for human consumption.

Low neck shots from the front can also cause much meat damage. The bullet kills the deer outright, but may travel on to re-enter the body alongside the spine, causing the loss of a fillet and maybe a haunch also.

Meat Spoilage and Bullet Choice

Meat spoilage is often cited as a reason for head/neck shots. I am aware that some game dealers will only take head-shot deer, which encourages unethical shots. A good heart/lung shot will cause minimal meat loss unless an explosively expanding bullet is used and fragments.

Throughout this discussion I have referred to a controlled expanding bullet. This is key to any shot in a given body area, more so than calibre, and will determine to a large extent if the deer runs far after the shot. The speed of a bullet also has a bearing on its performance and therefore meat damage. It's fair to say that the average velocity of a bullet from commercial non-magnum rounds mostly falls between 807 and 884m (2,650–2,900ft) per second. A bullet travelling much faster than this, probably light for calibre, has the potential to cause much damage unless of stout construction. A bullet leaving the rifle relatively slowly, meanwhile, may have slowed enough upon reaching a deer at longer range that it may not expand sufficiently for a good kill. This is the reason why a .308 hunting round will be in the region of 150–180 grains, for example, and a .270 calibre round will be 130–150 grains. These weights of bullet in each calibre will comfortably attain sufficient velocity. There are a lot of variables to consider in the world of ballistics, but the popular bullet weights of various cartridges on the gunshop shelf are there for good reason.

If the hunter is shooting deer exclusively in the head, close up in a deer park, for example, a more frangible round can be used, such as the Nosler Ballistic Tip or Hornady SST, among others, which will cause massive trauma to the skull and/or vertebra, ensuring a quick death. If used for heart/lung shots, these types of bullet can cause a very large wound channel, with bleeding along the separation between muscle groups, and much meat can be lost. It's not unusual to lose whole shoulders to this type of bullet if bone is contacted on the way through.

If the stalker is mainly taking heart/lung shots, however, a somewhat harder bullet can be used, such as a bonded soft point. This will mushroom, causing a decent wound channel, but will not be as explosive as the plastic-tipped bullets. Good kills can be achieved without much meat loss. However, if taking brain and spinal shots,

A non-bonded bullet entered at the lower site and came apart. Some exited at the second wound slightly higher up, the remainder turned and came to rest by the trachea, exposed when the animal was stuck.

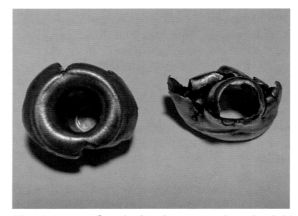

There is no sign of any lead in these recovered non-bonded bullets.

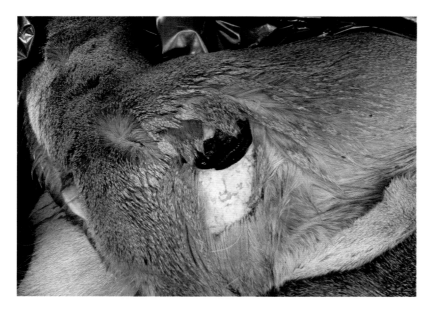

The entry wound on this roe is from a bullet that expanded too rapidly. The deer was killed on the spot, but there was much meat damage to the carcass.

Good bullet path and ideal expansion from a bonded heavier bullet: it took out the top of the heart but did not cause too much meat damage.

the stalker needs to be accurate, as the soft-point bullet does not send shards off in different directions as the ballistic tip variety can do – which, dare I say, can aid the slightly wayward shot.

I favour the harder, bonded bullets, as most shots I take are heart/lung and I don't like to waste any venison, having taken the animal's life, but consideration of terrain is another factor. Stalking in fields and woodland is relatively open, and a deer that runs 10 or 15 metres isn't going to be hard to find. In a very dense conifer plan-tation or in hilly areas the hunter may be faced with a long or difficult search and extraction if the deer runs after the shot, so meat damage may be of secondary concern to anchoring the deer to the spot. So in this sort of terrain a more rapidly expanding bullet aimed at the shoulders may suit the hunter best. As in many other areas of life, it is important to choose the equipment best suited for the occasion for a good and reliable outcome, and one size does not fit all situations.

Chapter 6

A Stalker's Year

My stalking year effectively starts on 1 August. This is for a number of reasons; the accounts and reports are given to the estates for the year ending 31 March, the end of the doe season, but little stalking is carried out over the summer. My remits are all cull-based management, so deer number reduction or maintenance is the primary objective, and deer are mostly left alone over this period. A stalker's year will mostly follow mine, if his or her lease covers a mixed area of arable, livestock and some woodland or coppice as found over most of England. Some variations will apply, but for the most part many stalkers will recognize the yearly pattern of activities.

It is said that one can stalk every month of the year in the UK, and while true, there are times when it's best to leave deer alone, both for their benefit and the stalker's, too.

AUGUST

August is the start of the long fallow buck, sika and red stag season, which runs to the end of April in England. It's an enjoyable time of the year, as stalking involves looking over the harvested fields for younger bucks or stags, grazing in the long evening period before night proper. It's not taxing compared to stalking during the rest of the year, because identification is easy: the whole of the animal is visible, not partly hidden by undergrowth as it would be in the woods. Further, if a cull animal is shot, the stalker can drive his vehicle straight to the carcass and load it up, since the landowner's crop has been removed. This is usually after dark by the time it is picked up, so placing a flashing head torch on the carcass after the shot ensures the return is straightforward – it's easy to lose even a large deer carcass in a big field at night.

The stalker wishing to make the most of the opportunities that this time of year has to offer will liaise closely with the contractor who cuts the estate's crop, aiming to be at each field the evening of harvest, and three or four evenings

Roe doe with yearling on stubble in August. This is a good time to count the deer on one's ground.

following, too. Deer don't seem to realize for quite a while that they are highly visible on the new stubble while they hoover up spilt grain. I have some high seats that look across open fields, and have been in one of them on numerous occasions while the combine is at the far end of a field, or in an adjacent one, and deer have emerged from the woods, investigating in the early evening. They are quite relaxed, as I have deliberately left them mostly alone for the four months prior to this over the summer, partly for this reason.

This approximately two- to three-week period before the stubble is ploughed back in gives an opportunity to count, in my case, roe and fallow. The fawns are up and about with their mothers by this time, so the stalker can get an idea of the doe cull that will be necessary later in the year, by observing if roe does have produced twins, or very occasionally triplets, or maybe it's been a poor year, and many of the fawns that are following does are single ones. Muntjac, on the other hand, are never keen on the fields, preferring to stay at the grassy margins and browsing.

An increasingly large part of my cull is fallow, and to shoot the required number I like to make a start as soon as possible on the young spikers and poor older bucks. If I can take some ten males of mainly a young age early in the season, that is 15 per cent of my fallow cull in a normal year. Come November I can then concentrate exclusively on the does. It is worth repeating that as most permissions require number reduction and control, does are the ones that reproduce, so are the more important sex (of any species) if this is to be achieved. A buck will remain a single deer all its life, while does, hinds and their female offspring will continue to replace any culled deer.

On other estates surplus roe bucks will already have been taken; it is considered excellent summer sport, and to call in a buck while the rut is on in late July to early August is often taken to be the height of the activity. Estates and lease-holders can derive a good income from selling the opportunity to shoot a mature, six-pointed roe buck to the numerous overseas hunters wishing to stalk in the beautiful English countryside. I may take a yearling or a couple of four pointers (a buck of around two to three years of age,

depending on local conditions) in August, even though they have been in season since April – but year after year I see good mature bucks coming through on my permissions, only for them to disappear over the summer. An early morning or evening foray on to an adjoining estate is often fatal for these deer.

Most animals taken at this time of the year are young, and I hang them in the fridge for a few days then butcher them into joints. This takes some of the pressure off the winter doe season, as my landowners put in requests for fillets or haunches just prior to Christmas. Having some good venison in the freezer means I'm always able to supply them, and don't have to target younger animals for them unnecessarily later in the year.

SEPTEMBER AND OCTOBER

These are quiet months for the stalker with a traditional mixed arable permission. As the fields are mostly brown earth, the stubble having been long since ploughed in and nothing new showing through to eat, there is no reason for deer to be in the open – and besides, the woods will have a dense abundance of undergrowth.

The October rut of red, sika and fallow is a further reason to leave the area quiet as, personally, I dislike shooting any males on their stands, preferring to leave them to their pleasures. It is a spectacle to watch from afar, though, particularly as the same stands are used year after year, so the resident stalker should have a good idea where this will take place. It's also a good opportunity to see mature bucks or stags, as these remain hidden for much of the rest of the year. Another reason to leave them be is that male venison pumped full of testosterone is not good eating; furthermore, shortly after the rut they will be in poor condition, with little reserves of fat, not having eaten for some time.

An exception to a break in stalking at this time is the stalker who oversees a plantation of saplings. Much new woodland has been planted across our country in recent years (*see* Chapter 10), and stalkers are often charged with protecting it. The less mature plantations can benefit from high seats placed at strategic points, as the

Stubble is quickly ploughed in nowadays; wild bird mix attracts only roe from the woods in September and October.

This sapling has been pushed over and the bark stripped bare by deer.

Maize cover crop targeted by fallow; this is the only food in the open that will tempt them out of the woods.

A chance shot at the occasional autumn fox presents an opportunity to help the gamekeeper.

lack of undergrowth makes culling deer along the rides a viable proposition. Deer will find their way into most fenced plantations, especially muntjac, who can squeeze through the narrowest of gaps under a strong fence. Roe follow, and bucks will damage much bark on young trees come spring when they are cleaning the velvet from their antlers. If plantations are unfenced but tubed, larger deer can reach the tips and will nibble at them, stunting growth. They can also push over young tubed saplings, making each one a complete loss to the landowner.

If a shoot operates on the ground, the game cover will require the stalker's attention, being the only crop in the open available to deer and therefore a magnet to their feeding forays. Traditionally planted maize is well liked by deer, and the shoot captain or gamekeeper will be quick to complain if much damage is done to the strips of crop. The gamekeeper will do his rounds often to check his pheasant poults, so deer learn to keep away until almost dark. I often take some foxes at this time, but this is just chance – I don't set out to target them deliberately, although the keeper is pleased if I do.

In this period I will make another check on high seats, cut any bramble back from the access paths, and trim branches that may have drooped, restricting the view from them. Some seats have netting to hide the occupant, so I ensure that all is serviceable and secure, replacing 'No unauthorized use' signs as necessary. The ability to approach seats quietly in darkness is a big part of a successful morning's stalk come winter.

In the run-up to the doe season there is an added advantage in leaving well alone, by allowing the deer to remain calm when they sense they are being approached. The first few deer shot in November will not be difficult, but thereafter they will steadily become more wary, and if overly targeted by the stalker they will only appear in the open at night, and will be gone by dawn.

Crab-apples are not liked by deer; they are left to rot.

NOVEMBER AND DECEMBER

The long-awaited doe season begins slowly in the woods (Scotland's doe season opens a few weeks earlier), as ferns do not die back early without a series of heavy frosts, of which we do not seem to have had many in recent years in southern England. Making use of high seats at this time by using a walker to gently move deer around the woods is a good idea. Even then, sometimes all that can be seen of them are flashes of brown or grey as they push past swaying ferns – certainly not enough for positive identification to enable the trigger to be squeezed.

I have some large old beech trees growing randomly in a few woods, and the mast (fruit) they produce in autumn attracts deer. These are good locations to find deer, either feeding there, or on their way to do so. Oak trees of course produce acorns, which are also attractive to deer; crab-apples however seem to be less favoured, and are left to rot on the wood or coppice floor.

Some stalkers have success with mineral licks,

but I have had mixed results. I've set up various flavours of lick block over the years on a metre-high stump about 80 metres from a high seat. Despite a clear view to it, I have never shot a deer while it made use of them, although these blocks are certainly used, judging from the slots around the stump and the diminishing size of the block itself.

Out in the grassy fields, cattle will have been moved indoors, so these areas become available to stalk. Early mornings seem to yield best results here. The stalker will try to take barren does early in the season, or yearlings that don't yet have fawns, but in truth any mature does are taken towards the end of November, their fawns are then shot also, as they often either stay in the open or return close to the culled mother inside fifteen minutes. They are generally of a decent weight, 11.3 to 12.7kg (25 to 28lb) field dressed for roe, enough for the game dealer to process, so are not wasted. I don't think anyone enjoys doing this, but the reality of deer number reduction is that they have to be taken out.

By mid-December the undergrowth is finally dying back and muntjac are more easily seen. It is well documented that the population mushroomed from around 2012 in many areas. Along with many other deer managers, my permissions collectively decided on a shoot-on-sight policy for this invasive species some years later. I then shot around thirty-plus a year, and the results were quite quickly realized; currently I am back to taking around sixteen a year after four years of the intensive cull policy. Unlike fallow, which will roam many miles and move on if unduly disturbed, muntjac are quite territorial so a local population can be controlled without too much external immigration.

From late November through much of December, winter inappetence can be experienced, where many stalkers find that deer just seem to disappear. In fact their bodies are adapting to the winter, slowing their metabolism to conserve body fat for the possibility of little food in the coming months. Deer lie up for long periods in sheltered spots and are thus not so visible, often until well after the shortest day (winter solstice), around the 21 December, when they start to move again due to lengthening daylight hours.

Christmas and New Year

At Christmas and over the New Year the estates I stalk have families in residence, so I take a break from around 23 December to 5 January. Social visitors and afternoon walks with dogs to wear off heavy meals do not sit well with deer stalking, so I restart after the New Year.

THE INFLUENCE OF THE WEATHER

Rain makes stalking very difficult, and I always try to avoid it if possible. Deer are not stupid, having thrived for many thousands of years, and will lie up until a storm passes. If pushed, they will jump up and bound off at the last moment when the stalker is nearby, which is not ideal for culling. However, if the stalker is patient, deer will move when the rain stops, and it is a good opportunity to take some in the woods, especially as water dripping from the trees can mask the sound of movement.

I stalk two or three times a week in the winter months, but will lay off if it is stormy and wet. Very high winds will also cause deer to lie up, but if a strong breeze prevails, it is helpful as it usually maintains its direction. In contrast a gentle breeze is fickle and can change direction, given a small hill or dale. One can be stalking into a breeze, round a corner and have it coming from behind. A cardinal rule is to stalk into the wind, because if you do not, any deer in front will be warned of your approach with their acute sense of smell.

Winter can produce some beautiful spells of bright, dry weather but this is not usually to the advantage of the stalker. Little rain means that the leaves underfoot are crisp and very noisy to stalk on. Coupled with a frost, such early mornings are, for me, a waste of time, and I find it is far better to allow the area to warm up a little, and start at 10 or 11am instead. Deer will stay bedded down in a heavy frost, and it is my experience that they will start to move later in the day, as frozen greenery isn't an appetizing meal. The urge to 'just get out there' is understandable, but sometimes it pays to stay in bed a few hours longer if hunting alone. My cull records show that over the years I have taken as many

Wide rides through the woods are useful for stalking, but not when the fallen leaves are dry and noisy underfoot.

deer from 10am to 2pm as in the early morning. Deer eat in four-hour cycles, lying up in between, so the advice to stalk at dawn and dusk does not always hold true. Deer learn quickly, and if targeted at these times only, they become more active at other times, and stalking during the day will produce results.

The downside to this is that by keeping going throughout the day the stalker becomes tired and loses concentration. It is therefore a good idea to take a short break now and again, to regain composure. I know I've caught myself going through the motions in stalking yet another coppice, but without paying attention. A deer has come into view unexpectedly and I

have not been ready. It is far better to stalk in intense bursts, with your eyes peeled and fully alert, picking your way quietly through the landscape.

On crisp days a walker or another stalker becomes invaluable, especially if stalking the more cautious fallow or sika. While one waits outside a wood, overlooking a known deer path and with a good backstop provided by the lie of the land or a high seat, the other can push gently through the undergrowth at a pace that does not alarm the herd unduly. The noise underfoot in fact helps to alert the deer from afar and gets them to move off quietly, hopefully so that they cross in front of the static rifle.

A hard frost on cover crops deters deer until later in the day.

Stalking Kidney Wood.

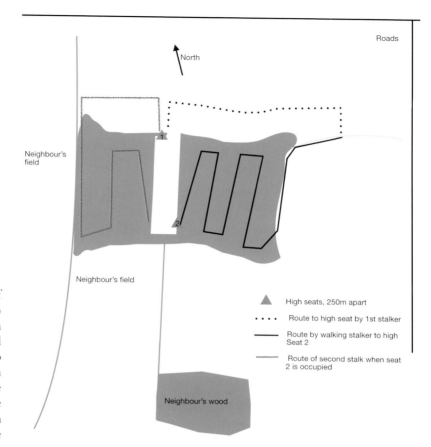

North

Roads

Neighbour's field

1

2

Neighbour's field

▲   High seats, 250m apart

· · · ·   Route to high seat by 1st stalker

——   Route by walking stalker to high Seat 2

——   Route of second stalk when seat 2 is occupied

Neighbour's wood

STALKING WOODS

The glade in the middle of Kidney Wood (*see* diagram) is an ideal spot for high seats. It is approached by the first stalker, who makes a wide circle out in the field; once in place, the second hunter stalks the wood, zig-zagging through to the glade, and takes the other high seat. The first stalker then circles round and walks through the second section of wood towards the occupied seat, which helps stop deer from leaving from the far side. This works extremely well and has produced culls of up to eleven deer in a morning, if not done too often.

Another small wood I have sits on the side of a hill, surrounded by fields. There is a definite preference for deer to leave the wood at a certain point, and it is facing this from about 80m that one stalker waits in a hedgerow, rifle on sticks but uncocked. The walking stalker is dropped off earlier, so he can circle widely around the opposite side and so enter the wood.

Any deer leaving have a good backstop, being on the side of a hill, and the walking gun will let the waiting stalker know when he is close to the exit so he can unload. It is a very effective stalking method, as operating alone deer often melt away unseen. The wind plays less of a role in success when stalking either type of wood, and noise isn't an issue either, because deer suddenly jumping up in front of the walking stalker gives the stalker stationed ahead an opportunity. The only caveat is for the walking stalker to move relatively slowly, as causing deer to run will spoil the drive, for in this country we do not shoot deer on the move, as they do in Europe.

JANUARY AND FEBRUARY

The eight-week period from the beginning of January to the end of February is when a good portion of the doe cull is carried out. The open woods, now mostly clear of undergrowth, look completely different from their appearance in early December. Deer have less choice of food, and the shoot's feed bins become very attractive, storing nutritious grain. Without stout support

Stalking a small hillside wood.

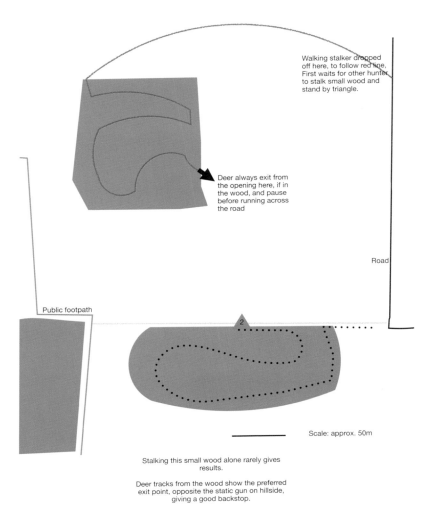

Walking stalker dropped off here, to follow red line, First waits for other hunter to stalk small wood and stand by triangle.

Deer always exit from the opening here, if in the wood, and pause before running across the road

Road

Public footpath

Scale: approx. 50m

Stalking this small wood alone rarely gives results.

Deer tracks from the wood show the preferred exit point, opposite the static gun on hillside, giving a good backstop.

One can help to minimize this by close focusing binoculars, then slowly increasing the in-focus distance, looking for branches between the rifle and deer that would normally be out of focus. The stalker can also do this with the side focus (parallax adjustment) on his rifle scope to some extent, if one is fitted.

MARCH

The bulk of the cull would hopefully be completed by the start of March, but prolonged bad weather can push the cull well into this month. On the one hand, days are getting longer, but having been chased around all winter, deer can be harder to approach. This can be compounded if the gamekeepers of nearby shoots are culling deer too, their season having finished at the end of January. Does are very pregnant at this time, and although the foetus is not viable (i.e. not able to live outside the womb), it looks almost fully formed, which is distasteful to some.

My take on this is that does are noticeably pregnant when carcasses are inspected internally by the New Year. Having being impregnated during the rut in late summer, the uterus contains a small but obvious foetus. If one is concerned about *potential* fawns, then the stalker logically

and wire surrounds, bins are pushed over by larger deer who then feast on the spilt contents. This can cause friction with the shoot, who want to keep feeding their birds so they don't wander off. It's a fine balance, for if the stalker pays too much attention to the cover crop, he or she can get the blame should the shoot have a poor day.

Longer, seemingly clear distances through the woods offer shots at greater ranges, but also the possibility of deflected bullets by unseen thin branches between the rifle and deer. I admit this has happened to me – a perfectly reasonable shot is taken, but the deer just stands there and then wanders off.

must refrain from culling does during the open season as nature will take its course and the doe will produce its offspring, which will not enable does to be culled. A viable foetus, on the other hand, will not occur until some weeks prior to the normal birthing period of late May to early June, so perhaps early May. Adopting this 'viable' position by the ethical stalker allows does to be culled during the current open season dates.

APRIL

By late March and into April I take just fallow bucks, which have another month in season. Given a mild winter, crops are around 60cm (2ft) high by mid-April. Fallow, red and sika like to be out on this, and given a warm day, lie up in the sun. Younger bucks and stags (spikers) will be among the does, or perhaps in smaller male groups, and it is certainly possible to cull some, although care needs to be taken not to cull does/hinds, which will greatly outnumber young bucks/stags in a mixed herd.

April is the start of the roe buck season, which runs out of kilter to other male deer. Younger bucks may not be out of velvet by the start of their season, though older, more mature examples usually are.

You can see a long way through the woods in late winter, but beware of branches between yourself and a shootable deer.

Young sika stag in a spring crop.

The bark has been rubbed off this young sapling by roe bucks.

Red stags are termed to be 'in tatters' when the strips of velvet cling on to the newly grown antlers, which is very descriptive, but the term doesn't seem to be carried across to other deer species. Trophy hunters may like to wait for some colour to develop on antlers, gained by rubbing against tree bark, but a plantation owner would rather the bucks were taken at the start of April to stop further fraying of younger trees.

MAY TO JULY

Many stalkers take a break during May to July, or at least reduce their visits to their ground just for the occasional look around and perhaps to take a younger buck that is considered suitable to cull. Professional stalkers are busy, however, up very early in the morning and out again for an evening stalk with clients for good roe bucks, of which the UK produces many. The run-up to the roe rut, starting late in July, is a good opportunity to see bucks chasing does for the chance to mate.

Females are giving birth from mid-May to early June, and the calves/fawns produced are hidden in long grass or woodland undergrowth. There is no reason to disturb them by stalking, but maintenance work on high seats can be carried out. Deer seem to know the difference between the movements of the hunter with a rifle and the relatively noisy works around seats and rides, so in my experience are not unduly alarmed by this.

Muntjac, having no close season, can be taken at this time of year, but grassy rides are now left longer between cuts for wild birds and insects to utilize. This can hide the little deer effectively, as all that can be seen of them is the humped back and a darting head. Muntjac mostly get a free ride through the summer, which goes some way to explaining their rising numbers.

In summer I catch up on personal equipment and rifle maintenance, producing some new cartridges for the seasons ahead. I prove them at the range and do some general practice towards the end of July, as it's surprising how quickly one becomes rusty by not shooting regularly for three months. Warm summer days are enjoyable at the range, and stalkers should embrace the opportunity to shoot at a variety of distances if possible. This rounds out the year nicely, as the following month it's back to the fallow bucks.

Professional stalkers aside, hunting as a recreation can grow wearisome if carried out relentlessly every week. The seasons change the look of the landscape dramatically, giving a new environment every couple of months – as shown by the images taken around my stalking grounds and reproduced at the beginning of each chapter – but whatever the conditions, the rest afforded to deer in between times of intense activity is good practice. I relate this to skiing – bear with me – for while I love to ski and look forward to my trips to the French Alps every winter, the enjoyment I get would be much less if I skied every week of the year: it would become ordinary. Many people I have met who live in the mountains are just occasional, fair weather skiers. The 'must get up there' drive in any weather soon settles down, and the locals often look for fresh snowfall and blue skies before pulling on their boots.

Re-locating and building high seats does not seem to bother deer during high summer.

To take this back to stalking, it would be a poor situation if the hunter declined to go during the peak times due to dull weather or sodden ground after much rainfall because of stalking burnout. I believe that taking a break during the year is a good part of why I still enjoy hunting after some twenty-five years of looking after the same estates.

Rides and field margins are left for insects and bees, hiding muntjac in the summer months.

Chapter 7

After the Shot, to the Larder

It is a truism that after the shot the real work starts. It can easily take a couple of hours to partially eviscerate, recover, transport, inspect and dress a carcass for the fridge in a hygienic and professional manner, then clean up afterwards. This chapter discusses these steps and the different approaches needed over challenging terrain and at different times of the year.

Going back a little to discuss events just prior to the shot of a chosen animal, one needs to remember to observe its behaviour. Is it acting normally, or is it drooling, lagging behind other deer in the herd or group, repeatedly licking itself, lame or wandering aimlessly around? These observations are highly important with regard to subsequent carcass inspection, as these symptoms are of course lost when the deer is killed. Noting such abnormalities can help a disease diagnosis (*see* Chapter 9, the section on chronic wasting disease).

INITIAL INSPECTION

When approached, the carcass needs to be appraised. Is it overly thin, or emaciated/poor with bones clearly showing through the hide, or is it nicely rounded? Young animals will not be plump as they have not yet matured, and in the depths of a hard winter a cull deer may well be underweight – but this may be normal given the conditions. Things to look out for are scouring or diarrhoea, an over-abundance of ticks indicating poor condition, nasal mucus, or unusual lumps and bumps anywhere on the carcass, including warble larvae, which may be under the skin on either side of the spine. Hooves and lips should not have sores (vesicles), which may indicate foot and mouth disease. Chapter 9 has more details of conditions.

BLEEDING

Assuming the deer is found dead, different approaches to dealing with the carcass will be necessary, depending on a number of factors. First the hunter must consider whether to bleed the carcass immediately. If neck or head shot, the

Approaching the dead deer: is anything unusual?

carcass needs to be bled as soon as possible, for the animal will have died through destruction of the brain or spinal injuries, which does not necessarily cause much blood loss. In this case arteries, muscles and organs will maintain blood pressure, which is released when the hunter 'sticks' the animal at the base of the neck in the jugular furrow, ideally using a 10cm (4in) blade. This will sever the jugular vein and carotid artery to effect a good bleed without going too deeply into the thoracic cavity.

Sticking can be done while the carcass is lying horizontally, but more blood will escape if it is hung by its back legs from a nearby tree, because although the heart will have stopped, gravity will drain the carcass of much blood. I never leave a neck- or head-shot deer for longer than fifteen minutes before I stick it, which can mean leaving a high seat mid-way through a morning or evening session to deal with a carcass, instead of waiting for other deer to appear.

This time limit is informed by experience in the abattoir, where animals are stuck well within thirty seconds of stunning, whether sheep, pig or bovine. If for some reason an animal were left for thirty minutes before being bled, inspectors would be viewing the carcass with suspicion. After processing, the carcass would be hung in the 'detained room' overnight to see if it were fit for human consumption after being allowed to drain. If the muscles were found to be overly bloody when incised, the carcass would be condemned. (*See* Chapter 9, 'Imperfect Bleeding'.)

There is discussion surrounding blood remaining in carcasses: Thornton and Gracey (1974), Pearson (1972) and Anon (1975) have questioned why the presence of sterile blood in a carcass should affect the keeping quality[1], as its presence doesn't spoil meat as was once previously thought. Gracey (2015) says that 'The extra blood retained by the poorly bled animal is retained mainly in the viscera and skin'.

However, in our context I'm talking about arteries, veins and organs full of blood, in a deer that is killed with *no* blood loss as opposed to one that is poorly bled. Perhaps it is a case of being 'visually repugnant' in that the meat is edible, but excessive blood oozing from cut surfaces is not appealing.

I know neck- or head-shot deer are sometimes brought to the larder some hours after death before being stuck to save spillage in the vehicle; personally I think this is not an acceptable practice. If the deer were heart or lung shot, the animal would have died primarily from blood loss. Much of this blood will still be inside the thoracic cavity, but crucially not in the muscle and circulatory system. It is reasonable to recover the deer when shot in this way, and either hang it vertically from a suitable tree and stick it, or transport it back to the larder and eviscerate it there, as long as this is within, perhaps, an hour or so.

The act of sticking in this scenario is more to do with letting blood drain from the thoracic cavity than from the body tissues, which would have taken place before the hunter had got to the carcass. Trials at the UK Meat Research Institute have shown that sheep bled in the horizontal position lose approximately 10 per cent more blood than those suspended vertically, an interesting parallel with deers which, when shot in the field, expire horizontally on the ground.

Hocked and stuck muntjac, awaiting collection.

Bearing this in mind, I believe a chest-shot deer would approach a similar level of blood loss as would the ewe or lamb at 75 per cent of available blood within fifty to sixty seconds of sticking[2]; this is because the heart is likely to continue pumping for a minute or two after the animal is shot, evacuating the carcass of much blood in the first seconds thereafter.

The time of year plays a part in how promptly it is necessary to expedite the stick and evisceration. In summer this really needs to be done as soon as possible before the rumen starts to blow with gases and makes opening the abdominal cavity difficult without cutting into it. In winter the hunter has more time before the stomach starts to swell. Many a cleanly shot carcass has been ruined by gut content contaminating the meat as a result of poor butchery skills.

RECOVERY

Recovery can take many forms, and the methods used depend to a large extent on the numbers being shot. One cannot hope to drag thirty large red deer a week out of a forest by hand and, conversely, just as a quad purchased to recover the occasional roe is not economic.

If the hunter is not able to drive the road transport vehicle directly to the carcass, the quad bike is often the most versatile means of getting to the scene without making deep ruts in very uneven, soft ground. Deer can then be lifted clear of the field or woodland floor, which is the most hygienic method. The carcass can be dragged manually with a rope to a ride then picked up by vehicle, but dragging the stuck carcass over mud, through water and no doubt animal excrement is not ideal due to contamination entering the stick wound and being picked up on the hide. In this scenario, a drag followed by bleeding is the way forwards.

Larger, heavier animals are often partly eviscerated (the stomach and intestines are removed) to reduce weight before recovery. This can allow the entry of much contamination, and a drag mat, bag or sled can be used to keep the carcass clean; the sled can be towed behind a quad to avoid heavy lifting. If shot on a steep hill, an electric winch mounted on a vehicle can be employed to

Dragging this muntjac along a grassy ride before evisceration will not cause contamination issues.

recover a carcass 50 metres or so, saving a lot of manual labour.

I have stashed a wheelbarrow in my largest wood, as vehicles are not permitted to enter the smaller rides. This both reduces manhandling and keeps the carcass clear of mud and ground water, a simple and effective recovery system. I keep a further barrow at another smaller permission, which produces five or six deer a year. It is less than 50 acres (20ha) but a little hilly. The barrow works very well here, too.

Once at the vehicle, smaller deer species are no problem to load, but sika, fallow and of course reds are problematic, being simply too floppy and heavy to manhandle alone into the back of a vehicle without risking back injury. Large southern reds are often winched on to a flatbed pickup truck or trailer using an A-frame or post with an arm. Mostly they will be eviscerated at this time too, over a large bucket, and left to drain for some minutes before laying them down to be taken to the fridge.

A post and arm are excellent for the evisceration and handling of larger species.

For fallow I have a simple 5:1 pulley attached to my roof bar, which allows the deer to be easily raised, pausing to allow the carcass to drain; the front legs and neck are then lifted into the lipped watertight tray for transportation.

STICKING AND EVISCERATION

There are many slightly different ways to stick and eviscerate a deer. I'll describe my method, which may or may not suit the reader. It is adapted from a method used historically in abattoirs for cattle, before vertical line processing was introduced.

When sticking, the deer is lying horizontally on the ground, its legs to the left when viewed from the tail, as pictured here. I stand facing away from the carcass, one heel under the chin, the other at the sternum, pushing the front legs away from the neck, which, importantly, stretches the skin and makes it easier to cut. Bending down, I work between my legs. I insert the knife under

the chin and run it back towards the jugular furrow (the depression before the sternum). I pull the skin back and run the knife along the side of the trachea (the windpipe). This frees it from connective tissue, and the oesophagus (food-pipe) at the rear can be separated by hand and cut near the larynx. With younger animals, the outer sheath of muscle can be scraped back about 2cm with a fingernail; in older deer a knife will be needed to mark around it, then the muscle sheath scraped back with the back of the knife. The oesophagus is then simply knotted, held in place at the separated muscle. A gentle tug will help free the oesophagus from connective tissue as it runs along the trachea inside the body. Here the windpipe can either be cut off close to the body, or be left in place.

The knife is then pushed into the jugular furrow at an angle of around 45 degrees to cut the carotid arteries and jugular vein; blood will then run out. The stalker can keep his hands clean, as all the necessary work has already been completed in this area.

Moving to the side of the body, I place one foot behind the rear legs, hooking the top one behind my own leg, my other foot placed alongside the spine. This pulls the carcass over on to its back a little, exposing the belly. If a female I catch hold of some skin below the udder and cut off a patch up to the inside of the rear legs, including the udder. If a male I hold the penis at the end and cut a patch back towards the testicles, removing all at the start of the rear leg muscle. Some stalkers leave the penis and testicles in situ, to be removed later, but this is not necessary. Urine will not run out when severed, as what is left of the penis will naturally pull back and seal itself. Others like to remove the penis completely, opening the skin and chasing the penis to its origin back inside the pelvis. However, this exposes meat to contamination and the drying effects of air in the fridge. I've never seen this done in any abattoir, so see no advantage in doing so with deer. The stomach can then be cut open, from the udder/penis end to the sternum. Some use a gut hook for this, to avoid nicking the rumen, resulting in green content contaminating the meat.

With the feet still in the same position, the rumen and intestines will spill out, *away* from the hunter. Reaching inside, the spleen can be located

The process of sticking on the ground.

on the upper side of the body near the liver, and pulled free of connective tissue, together with the rumen. The oesophagus becomes exposed as the whole is eased out, and can be gently pulled through the centre of the diaphragm, the knotted end intact. A knife may be necessary to cut the connective tissue to the liver and kidney area in an older animal.

The only tissue connecting the gut to the carcass will now be the large intestine going towards the rectum. Some like to tie this off in two places and cut in the middle to seal in the content. Unless completely filled with pellets, I use two fingers to drag the few pellets inside to the gut end, and cut. Nothing escapes in my experience.

This is all that is necessary before arriving at the larder, but feet and head are usually removed prior to lifting into a vehicle. Describing how to mark around the front and rear legs to crack the appropriate joints is not precise in print; it is best to allow an experienced hunter to demonstrate how to do this, and something else to be learnt if the new stalker is out with a professional guide. However, I do think there is no shame in sawing off the legs below the joints!

Removing the head from the atlas joint causes problems for some hunters. I believe this is often due to connective tissue remaining around the area, stopping separation. I make sure the throat area is severed back to the bone, between the head and larynx. I then hold an ear, cutting at the base of it all around the back of the head. Working slowly, pulling hard against the weight of the body to expose each cut, the joint becomes exposed. At some point the joint gives, and the knife can be inserted into the joint and it can be opened by cutting connective tissue. If the hunter starts hacking at bone, something is amiss; the joint will separate if all surrounding tissue has parted and the other hand is pulling hard.

Evisceration of the stomach and intestine.

HEAD AND INTESTINE INSPECTION

This is a good time to inspect the head and intestinal nodes for infection, most notably tuberculosis (TB), before the exposed tissue gets dirty by contacting the ground. The images here show the sites to inspect on a 'normal' set of nodes. It is important to be familiar with the range of normal, so the abnormal can be recognized. Normal nodes can range from being large and leaking fluid when cut in the young animal, to dry and smaller, darker nodes in the mature deer. All indicate that no disease is present in them. Meanwhile, images in Chapter 9 show the abnormal, TB-infected condition.

Tuberculosis is easily spotted: the lymph

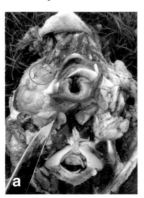

Three sets of head lymph nodes. (a) Knife pointing at one retropharyngeal; the other is 2cm to the right. The submaxillary gland is further forward, circled red, near the angle of the jaw. (b) Knife pointing at the salivary gland, often mistaken for a lymph node. The submaxillary gland is circled red. This gland often goes missing when the head is removed. (c) Knife pointing at a parotid lymph node, located to the rear of the massater (cheek) muscle, circled. (d) The other parotid gland can see seen; note the ear canal close by, circled.

Mesenterics in a young and an older animal.

nodes are enlarged, and when cut a greenish pus will ooze, or can be of a pale yellow and cheesy consistency if more historic. Bovine tuberculosis is a notifiable disease and needs to be reported to the relevant authorities. If Johne's disease is present, the intestines will show different abnormalities.

If nothing is to be left in the field, the inspected intestine, feet and head are bagged, along with the rumen, which is cut open and emptied of contents on site. It is often interesting to see what the deer have been feeding on. The content can indicate where the herd have been spending their time, perhaps in a clover field or in the woods, hoovering up acorns for example.

EVISCERATING THE VERTICAL CARCASS

Many stalkers prefer to eviscerate a hanging carcass, which, on balance, produces a cleaner carcass. I find it easier to prepare the carcass for this by first sticking, loosening and tying the oesophagus, removing the udder/penis and sawing the sternum (as described in the previous section). When vertical, the rectum is cut around, then all the hunter has to do is open the abdominal cavity down to the sternum. The organs will then be removable, firstly the rectum and large intestine, then the small intestine and rumen. Care needs to be taken, as the weight of a full rumen can cause it to fall free of the carcass, breaking the oesophagus at the point where it goes through the diaphragm, and allowing green content to contaminate the cavities.

The hunter can remove the liver, keeping it clean and separate if it is to be eaten later, then cut around the diaphragm, freeing the lungs from the spine by sliding the knife down the rear. The heart, incased in the pericardium, has a little connective tissue inside the sternum, but easily pulls away. Having previously freed the trachea, the lungs and heart are removed. Some hunters like to use a spreader bar to access the pluck (heart, liver and lungs, complete), especially on larger deer. The organs and the cavity itself are inspected for abnormalities. This includes the

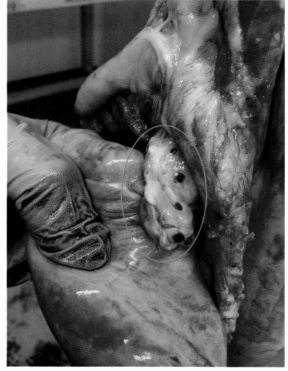

A normal deer liver. The portal lymph node is circled in green. The portal opening, cut to inspect for fluke, is circled in blue. The tenuicollis tracking is circled in red.

Left bronchial lymph node, under the aortic arch. Mediastinals run down between the lungs. The dark spots are haemal lymph nodes; they appear to act as small spleens, and are also found in the lumbar and pelvic regions.

liver and portal node attached to it and the lungs, the bronchial and mediastinal nodes.

A full list of possible conditions is found in Chapter 9.

SHOULD THE CAVITIES BE SWILLED WITH WATER?

In a controlled abattoir setting, removing blood with water has mostly been stopped, the carcass remaining dry at all times. However, a shot deer is, I feel, a little different, and I carry some clean, potable water in 2-litre containers. A little lightly sprinkled into the body cavity immediately after evisceration will wash most blood away, and if the carcass is left to drain for a short while, it will be clean. If there is no blood, there is no need to wash.

Any spilt gut content should be treated differ-

ently. This may look as if it is washed away, but bacteria will remain, so if a little has contacted the body tissue it should be trimmed off, being careful not to spread contamination by using the knife again elsewhere on the carcass without cleaning it first.

Allowing the carcass to drip for some minutes, perhaps while a vehicle is brought to the scene, keeps much blood out of the transportation tray in which the carcass will lie. It is beneficial to have a raised grid that the deer lies on, which allows blood run through to pool below, separated from the carcass (*see* image on page 117).

Back at the larder the deer is hung in the chiller on a gambrel. This separates the legs, aiding cooling. I leave the kidneys and associated fat in the carcass to stop the fillets from drying out, especially if the carcass will hang for a week or more. While the fat is still warm, the hunter

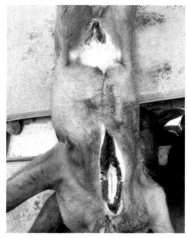

Removing the udder or penis and testicles, and sawing the brisket prior to hoisting the carcass vertically, helps with evisceration.

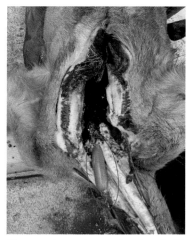

The oesophagus loosened and tied off (circled).

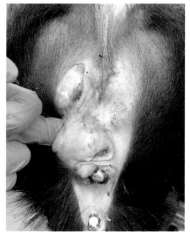

Jointing the tail and freeing the rectum is the first job when the carcass is hoisted.

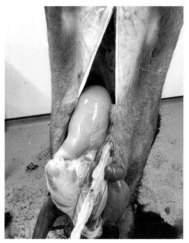

With the anus and connecting large intestine pulled down (circled in blue), the stomach, intestines and pluck are easily removed.

Care is needed to ensure that the oesophagus (circled in blue) does not break under the weight of a full stomach on removal.

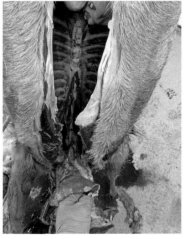

Cut round the diaphragm, then the heart, lungs and liver can be pulled down and out through the split brisket.

can cut into the kidneys just enough to peel back their protective membrane to check their condition; they should be a shiny dark brown colour (*see* Chapter 9). I then pop them back into their casing if they are quite healthy.

Many carcasses I see at my game dealer are split open at the pelvis through to the bone, or the aitch bone is sawn through. Perhaps this is done to aid the removal of the back passage, but

with a little knowledge of technique this can be avoided. It could also be thought to aid cooling of the carcass, but it isn't necessary. It exposes muscle both to the atmosphere, which dries it, and also to contamination, and this portion will need to be trimmed off at the butchery stage, which is a waste of prime meat. Sheep carcasses are not cut open while hanging whole in commercial cutting plants; the legs are only

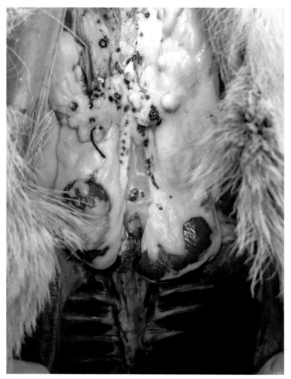

The kidneys and fat are left in this roe doe as they protect the fillets from drying out while the carcass is in the chiller.

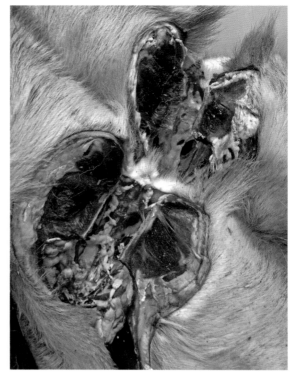

Roe legs split through the aitch bone; this exposes the meat to drying and contamination.

split when breaking the whole carcass down, for the same reason.

HOW LONG TO HANG?

A good deer fridge will easily keep carcasses in excellent condition for at least two weeks, as it will keep the humidity low. I set mine at 4°C, which goes a long way in stopping surface mould growing on exposed meat, but I see little benefit in hanging for longer than a week unless waiting to transport to the dealer.

A carcass hanging in a cold garage will need to be attended to within a few days, as the temperature will fluctuate between day and night, probably above the recommended 7°C unless it is a really cold spell. In summer, without a fridge the carcass should be covered in a muslin cloth to stop flies laying eggs, then one just needs to wait for rigor mortis to set in, perhaps overnight, before skinning and jointing. In this situation the

carcass will be for home consumption only (*see* Chapter 8 for selling on to a game dealer).

Cold shortening will not be an issue to most stalkers, as deer shot in the field will be well on their way to being sufficiently cooled before they get to a fridge, but it is something to be aware of. Cold shortening can happen to a fresh carcass if it is immediately placed in a very efficient cold fridge, without a period of slow cooling in between times. This leads to a contraction of muscles before normal rigor mortis sets in, due to the pH being above 6.2 and adenosine triphosphate (ATP) still present, resulting in tough venison. The mixing of already cooled carcasses with warm ones in a chiller is also to be avoided, for the same reason.

SKINNING

There are many ways to remove the skin of a deer. It is traditionally carried out on a cradle, the carcass lying on its back, but this method better suits the still warm, flexible carcass prior to rigor mortis, as the legs are still easily moved.

The carcass is suspended vertically by the hocks in the chiller, and it is best to skin it in this position when it is cold. Starting at the haunches, the knife should be inserted under the skin, the blade away from the meat when cutting, so contamination on the hide is not transferred to the exposed meat. Some stalkers use a gut hook to 'rip' open skin, allowing the meat to be protected from the usually pointed blade that can easily pierce the meat. The skin is then pulled down towards the shoulders and neck. This helps keep contamination to a minimum, as the best meat, the rear legs and saddle, are above the bullet holes with associated inter-muscular blood, which will seep downwards, away from those prime cuts. The image shows the minimal cuts necessary; further easing with a knife may well be needed, but everyone seems to have a different favoured way. As long as the skin can be removed cleanly and without much hair adhering to the exposed meat, one way is as good as another.

Most deer skin can be removed by pulling, or inserting a fist between the skin and 'velm' – the membrane covering the meat – and punching outwards. This is an acquired technique, again best demonstrated visually. Day courses of butchery techniques are run by the BDS and BASC, amongst other organizations, and are to be recommended.

'Best practice' shows the carcass, at the end of skin removal, as ready for the butcher's shop window, the operative rightly proud of his or her skills in presenting a perfectly skinned carcass. However, venison carcasses are not put on show, but are normally jointed immediately, so if the velm, fat or part of the flank comes away from the carcass when the skin is removed, it doesn't matter, as the various joints of meat will not be affected. The novice shouldn't worry unduly about this happening, but should concentrate instead on keeping contamination to an absolute minimum.

Some deer are harder to skin than others, cold muntjac being the most difficult, for some reason. I tend to skin these while they are still warm, which is much easier, and hang them for

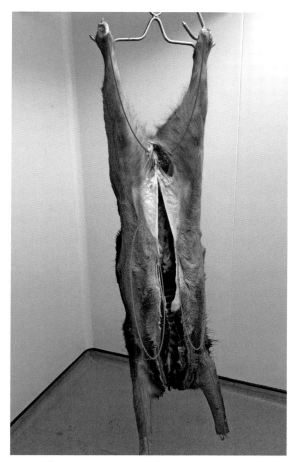

Minimal cuts are necessary to skin a carcass (in blue). Some easing with a knife may be necessary around the flanks and rib areas (circled in red).

just a further day before jointing. A deer carcass has significantly less fat than domesticated animals, so will dry out when in a fridge for even just a few days after skinning, while a lamb or side of beef will not, as it is protected by its fat. This is the basis for keeping wild game 'in the fur' in the first place.

BASIC BUTCHERY

With the skin off, the hunter can see the extent of blood seepage around the carcass if the deer were heart or lung shot. If a shoulder is badly damaged, for example, it is often easier to remove this and set it aside before jointing the better cuts. This reduces the chance of making a mess, and it can be dealt with at the end of the session when other, clean cuts have been bagged and refrigerated.

The forequarter is marked around the fourth or fifth rib back from the neck, and sawn through. The top of the fillets behind the kidneys run up past the point at which the saddle is sawn, so these are removed first. Two cuts either side of the spine will free them, and they can then be easily removed. The ribs are cut around 15cm (6in) parallel with the spine on either side; the brisket, having little recoverable meat, is discarded. Laying the saddle down, the two sirloins can be removed close to the bone.

Joints are double bagged to help prevent freezer burn, then labelled and dated for home consumption.

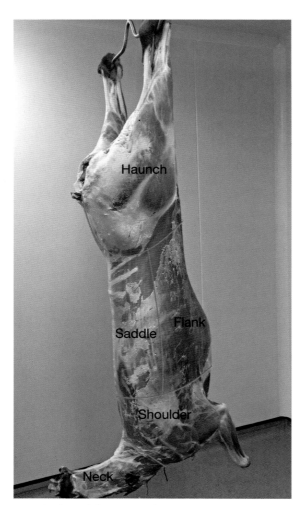

A nicely skinned deer carcass, but it's not going on show. The primal butchery joints are shown in red.

The legs (haunches) are sawn through and can be left whole, or part boned and tied, or completely boned and rolled or, if from a larger species, broken down into the various muscle groups for roasting, or cut up for leg steaks.

A full 45cm (17.5in) bone saw is the best size in the larder. It can also be used to saw through the sternum during initial evisceration, and for removing legs. Smaller push/pull saws can be used for the sternum and work efficiently, but I wait until the carcass is at the larder before cutting through any bone, so use my larger saw for everything.

After processing the better cuts, the next job is to deal with the shoulders, which are often bloodied. If not, they can be boned and rolled, but usually I cut them up, finishing with two piles of meat, best diced and straggly, perhaps a few bloodied scraps, but with no bone fragments. The diced is bagged for stews and casseroles, together with any decent-sized pieces left from the haunches and saddle. The scraps are 'dog meat', for animals fed in that manner, and are therefore not wasted.

If the various cuts and joints are to be frozen, I label, then double bag them to help prevent freezer burn. It is a shame to go through all the effort and processes to have meat spoiled due to insufficient packing. I label and date each piece, so nothing stays in the freezer for months on end.

It is more efficient to skin and butcher a number of deer at the same time, as then you only have to clean up once. I have space to skin and hang three carcasses without them coming into contact with each other, avoiding the risk of cross-contamination, so end up with six legs, six sirloins and perhaps 3kg (7lb) of best quality diced meat. The fridge, table, knives and floor are cleaned with hot water and a little detergent, then allowed to air dry, ready for the next carcasses to enter.

OF FRIDGES AND CHILLERS

When back at the place of storage (I'll call it the larder, but it could in fact be a garage) there is a variety of paths to go down. The stalker may have a game facility, a large fridge, a converted corner-shop cold drinks cooler, or just a muslin cloth to keep flies off the carcass overnight until it can be skinned and jointed when it is set the next day. It's a numbers game: if dealing with two hundred carcasses a year, cutting up and selling joints, then a game facility will be required in order to store and process the venison legally. Costs start at £30,000, so a considerable investment, plus the site, plumbing, drainage and electrical hookups. (*See* Chapter 8 for legislation regarding this.)

The next tier down is the purpose-built stainless-steel game fridge. These cost around £3,000 and can easily hold six roe or four/five large fallow on two internal rails. They have a footprint of 1 × 1m; I have a robust German-built one with the compressor sitting on top, well out of the way of a good wash and flush to keep it spotless. At the end of a long day culling deer in winter, or a very late finish in summer on bucks, it's good to be able to hang the day's kill, finish for the evening and go home for a well earned rest.

It can be hard to justify £3,000 for a fridge if only six or eight deer are shot in a year, as is the case with many stalkers, perhaps a few bucks and some does in winter. Often does can be hung in a garage, as the temperature can be cold enough to allow this for a few days, as long as it is below 7°C. In summer, bucks cannot be kept cool enough without refrigeration, so require either a trip to the dealer immediately, or to be processed within a few hours of shooting, as previously discussed.

Faced with this limited hanging time, there are many converted second-hand commercial drinks fridges or tall domestic fridges in use – those with an internal fan are best. The shelves are removed and a bar is solidly fixed internally near the top. Capable of keeping a couple of roe or a young fallow cool, they provide a solution for the occasional stalker who shoots during the week and needs the weekend to process the venison for his

Professional chiller for larger throughput.

A six-deer fridge in a container. Hot water, a freshwater hose and a lifting hoist over a tray makes for easy cleaning; it drains into a portable liquid waste container.

or her freezer. High internal humidity is often an issue with these units, and for that reason it's not always possible to hang carcasses for extended periods without surface mould growing, unlike the professional chillers which manage humidity. I stress that this low-cost solution is applicable for venison to be home consumed only. I doubt very much whether such a set-up would be acceptable if registering as a food business with the stalker's local council, for reasons of lack of space around the carcass, difficulty in keeping the unit clean, and the aforementioned humidity control.

If any deer are going to the dealer, they are part of a product chain that is to be sold eventually, so a more professional set-up is necessary to keep everything legal, and registering as a food business is part of this process (*see* Chapter 8).

IN CONCLUSION

This chapter serves to show that the actual stalking of deer is only a part of the hunting process. After the shot, much time can be spent by the novice in preparing the carcass. A good practical course will help prepare the new hunter, and save him or her much time and wasted effort when the successful stalk has ended, enhancing their enjoyment of the activity from start to freezer.

Chapter 8

Registering as a Food Business

Deer stalking is not the unregulated simple pastime it once was, as noted in other chapters in this book – obtaining leases, firearms legislation, risk assessment and insurance are now areas of concern for the hunter in today's world. Selling carcasses in the skin has long attracted official attention, such that it has been a legal requirement since 1 January 2006 to register as a food business and comply with Regulation (EC) 852/2004 and Regulation (EC) 853/2004, the EU food hygiene regulations. This has slowly been gaining traction, and a hunter taking deer carcasses to a game dealer needs to register, becoming a food business operator, be a 'trained hunter', and also be familiar with the hygiene regulations applicable, although there are exemptions, noted below.

DEER STALKING: A 'PRIMARY PRODUCTION ACTIVITY'

The EU food hygiene regulations regard the shooting or hunting of wild game for human consumption as a 'primary production activity'. Therefore a hunter acting alone or as part of a shooting party is a primary producer, if all he does is eviscerate and leave the carcass in the skin. What the stalker then does determines if he or she needs to register as a 'food business operator' or not, and which regulations apply. There are four scenarios the part-time stalker could find him or herself in, summarized as follows:

- The hunter who shoots just a few deer per year for home consumption only. This includes venison given to friends and family, relying on a hunter's exemption from the regulations,

the key point being that the product is not for sale. There is no requirement to register.
- The hunter who supplies small quantities of game *in the fur* to the final consumer, or to local retailers who supply the final consumer. Registration as a food business is required, but the game will not be subject to the requirements of Regulations 852/2004 or 853/2004. However, the hunter has obligations elsewhere, having to comply with the Food Safety Act 1990 'not to place unsafe foods on the market', and Regulation 178/2002, which covers traceability. More of this later. The exemption from Regulations 852/2004 and 853/2004 comes from the 'small quantities' clause.
- The hunter who supplies small quantities of *game meat* to the final consumer or to local retailers. The difference here is in processing the carcass past the primary producer stage of being 'in the fur'. The hunter will be required not only to register as a food business, but he or she will also be subject to regulation 852/2004 and will have a HACCP-based food-safety management plan in place (*see* later in this chapter). The requirements are adapted because of the 'small quantities' exemption clause, and some leeway is given for temporary premises on an individual basis.
- The hunter who supplies the game dealer, or an approved game-handling establishment (AGHE), either directly (field to dealer) or via a holding chiller belonging to the estate or stalker. Many stalkers fall into this band, myself included, and registration is required. The hunter needs to become a 'food business operator', and the premises and vehicle transporting the carcasses must comply with all

hygiene regulations, as the hunter is part of a supply chain of a product that can ultimately end up for sale by a third party in unlimited quantities.

REGISTRATION

Registration as a food business operator is done through one's local authority, by contacting the Environmental Health Department. I spoke to an environmental health officer (EHO) in Dorset who had given a talk under the BASC

Purpose-built larder with two entry points. Note the smooth concrete apron with drainage channel for easy cleaning.

umbrella to stalkers in her area about registering. Their office opinion is that it would give them a starting point in tracing poaching incidents and food-poisoning outbreaks. When dealing with EHOs in my previous job as a meat inspector I found them to be pragmatic rather than officious. I don't sense any hidden agenda in wishing to regulate every minute detail, which is often the public's concern when local or national government gets involved. It's a mechanism that when in place is left alone, but gives the officers somewhere to start when deemed necessary by outbreaks of food poisoning, which seems wholly reasonable to me.

Each council operates differently, and many stalkers will get an inspection of their premises, others just a phone call, or they may be required to send in images of the set-up. But there should be no nasty surprises, as there is a national guideline that all should follow: *The Wild Game Guide*.[1] It is thirty-eight pages long and mainly written in plain English. The legal status of the guide makes plain that:

> …it cannot cover every situation, and you may need to consider the relevant legislation itself to see how it applies in your circumstances. If you follow the guidance it will help you to comply with the law. Businesses with specific queries may wish to seek the advice of their local enforcement authority. (p.8)

As discussed at the end of this chapter, it is always best to enquire before committing to a plan of action. The observations I take from *The Wild Game Guide* here apply to deer only, although the guidance includes information about squirrels, wild boar, hares, rabbits and wild birds.

Deer carcasses in an estate chiller; plenty of space around the carcasses ensures that they are brought down to temperature efficiently.

Grey Areas

Of the four situations applicable to the hunter, the second and third situations, concerning the 'small quantities' exemption clause, cause most confusion. The second allows the primary producer (the stalker) to sell a number of carcasses to small local retailers, such as a local butcher or a pub, or directly to the final consumer, without having to comply with the full EU regulations. Many mistake this with the first situation, and wrongly believe that registration is unnecessary. This is a way for the poacher and unhygienic operator to sell their venison, for they and their customer base believe they can operate freely without restriction.

The differences between the second and third scenarios can be seen in the boxes. Primary products (game in the fur) are exempt from 852/2004 and 853/2004, but game meat is only exempt from 853/2004, meaning the producer of even small quantities of venison has to comply with 852/2004, general hygiene. This covers temperature control, HACCP, and hygienic transport both while in fur and in the later delivery of meat.

The specifics of 853/2004 include health marking, storage, transport, microbiological and temperature criteria for foodstuffs, and the structural and hygiene requirements of cutting plant facilities. These do not apply to food business operators dealing in small quantities, but are directed at larger commercial plants and slaughterhouses.

For home-consumed venison no registration is needed.

Even if exempt from the food hygiene rules, the hunter is still operating as a food business, therefore registration is required, and he or she is subject to the wide-ranging Regulation 178/2002. This covers the entire chain from primary production through distribution and retail, in that food should not be injurious to health. It also requires traceability, at all stages of production, processing and distribution, so the hunter always needs to comply with this, unless for private domestic use.

Further, the hunter, in supplying small quantities in the fur, also needs to comply with the Food Safety Act 1990. The Act does not cover hygiene specifically, but under point 12 (*see* box)

Regulation (EC) 852/2004: on the hygiene of foodstuffs

General Provisions
Article 1
Scope:
2. This Regulation shall not apply to:
(a) primary production for private domestic use;
(c) the direct supply, by the producer, of small quantities of primary products to the final consumer or to local retail establishments directly supplying the final consumer;

Source: www.legislation.gov.uk/eur/2004/852

Regulation (EC) 853/2004: specific hygiene rules for food of animal origin

Scope:
3. This Regulation shall not apply in relation to:
(a) primary production for private domestic use;
(c) the direct supply, by the producer, of small quantities of primary products to the final consumer or to local retail establishments directly supplying the final consumer;
(e) hunters who supply small quantities of wild game or wild game meat directly to the final consumer or to local retail establishments directly supplying the final consumer.

Source: www.legislation.gov.uk/eur/2004/853/ introduction

Regulation (EC) 178/2002: the General Food Law Regulation

Aim and scope:
3. This Regulation shall apply to all stages of production, processing and distribution of food and feed. It shall not apply to primary production for private domestic use or to the domestic preparation, handling or storage of food for private domestic consumption.

Food safety requirements:
1. Food shall not be placed on the market if it is unsafe.
2. Food shall be deemed to be unsafe if it is considered to be:
(a) injurious to health;
(b) unfit for human consumption.

Article 18
Traceability:
1. The traceability of food, feed, food-producing animals, and any other substance intended to be, or expected to be, incorporated into a food or feed shall be established at all stages of production, processing and distribution.
2. Food and feed business operators shall be able to identify any person from whom they have been supplied with a food, a feed, a food-producing animal, or any substance intended to be, or expected to be, incorporated into a food or feed. To this end, such operators shall have in place systems and procedures which allow for this information to be made available to the competent authorities on demand.

Source: www.legislation.gov.uk/eur/2002/178

The Food Safety Act 1990 – A Guide for Food Businesses

(2009 Edition)

11. The Act applies to all types of food businesses.
12. Your main responsibilities under the Act are:
to ensure you do not include anything in food, remove anything from food, or treat food in any way which means it would be damaging to the health of people eating it;
to ensure that the food you serve or sell is of the nature, substance or quality which consumers would expect;
to ensure that the food is labelled, advertised and presented in a way that is not false or misleading.
15. The Act covers activities throughout the food distribution chain, from primary production through distribution to retail and catering.

Source: The Food Safety Act 1990 – A Guide for Food Businesses, Food Standards Agency.

it could be argued that 'treating food in a way [that is] damaging to … health' would include a lack of hygiene.

Defending a charge brought under the Act can be made by citing due diligence, demonstrating that the supplier has taken all reasonable precautions to avoid the offence – but this is a matter for the courts to decide 'on balance of probability', whether such precautions were within the law.

A big question hanging over these pieces of legislation with regard to the part-time stalker is, how much does 'small quantities' mean, before the full regulations need apply? Three carcasses a year, three a month, or perhaps three a week? The guidance notes say 'Small quantities is regarded as self-defining because demand for in-fur or in-feather carcasses from final consumers and local retailers is limited' – but that is not at all helpful.

The BDS and BASC were also cagey about stating a number when asked, reiterating that it's a rather grey area. I would hazard a personal guess at twenty a year, as that means less than two a month, which seems manageable and wouldn't constitute a profitable business – but I could be wrong. Perhaps the hunter's local environmental health officers can help, but as they have access to the same rules that we have, they may not be in a position to offer more guidance.

The EU's Definition of 'Local'

'Local' is defined as one's own county that the facility is in, plus the greater of either the neighbouring county, or a 30-mile extension from one's own county border – but never beyond the UK unless supplying from Northern Ireland to the Republic of Ireland. When the supplying establishment is located in the Scottish islands, 'local' is interpreted as anywhere within Scotland. However, direct supply to the final consumer is not restricted by geography, and orders via the internet or mail can be sent country wide. Collections can be made from those arriving from outside the local area also.

Differences in Scotland

If a stalker processes carcasses for home consumption, or if he or she gifts venison, there is no requirement to be licensed. But Scottish law requires anyone selling venison to have a venison dealer's licence (VDL). If, for example, a butcher buys in venison, he will not be required to be licensed, only the supplier. However, if the stalker or estate is selling only to an approved game dealer, no licence is required, as the dealer will have a VDL. Licences are issued by the local council and are valid for three years. Licensed venison dealers must maintain records of purchases and receipts of venison, and these are open to inspection by the Deer Commission for Scotland.

In selling small quantities of either in-the-fur or 'cut' venison (again, the numbers or the amount are not specified), as allowed in the rest of the UK, a licence needs to be applied for. The stalker must follow hygiene rules and have a HACCP plan in place.

The Trained Hunter

Deer carcasses destined for the AGHE need to be examined by a 'trained person', someone who has sufficient knowledge of the pathology of wild game, and of the production and handling of wild game meat after hunting, to undertake an initial examination of carcasses on the spot. If no abnormal characteristics are found during the examination, nor abnormal behaviour observed before killing, and if there is no suspicion of environmental contamination, a numbered declaration stating this must be attached to the animal's body: the 'game tag'.

When supplying carcasses to an AGHE, at least one person of a hunting team must have this knowledge. The carcasses do not need to be accompanied by any viscera removed as part of normal hunting practice, but the operator of an AGHE may initially wish to see proof of the training or certification of the trained person certifying the carcasses. If no trained person

Deer at a game dealer are delivered chilled and tagged, maintained at 4°C until they are skinned and processed.

were available to carry out the initial examination of the bodies of wild game, animals may still be sent to an AGHE, but must be accompanied by the head (except for tusks, antlers or horns) and all the viscera (the organs of the thoracic, abdominal and pelvic cavities), except for the stomach and the intestines. The accompanying viscera must be identified as belonging to a given animal.

Training for the Deer Stalker

A deer stalker is recognized as a 'trained hunter' if he or she has passed the widespread introductory DSC 1 course, as it has been incorporated in the award since December 2005. Other qualifications are available from LANTRA, leading to a certificate in Large Wild Game Meat Hygiene. The National Gamekeepers' Organisation runs suitable courses, as does The Scottish Gamekeepers Association.

I disagree absolutely that anyone can be thoroughly competent in spotting diseases after completing one of the basic courses, but that's the law, and the diligent stalker wanting to do the right thing is at least on the path to producing venison that is fit to enter the food chain, keeping him- or herself within the law. Despite the regulations outlined above, stalkers are very lightly regulated here in the UK, and by being qualified and following the guidelines of fairly basic hygiene procedures, we can avoid the need for further legislation being forced upon us.

Not believing that the training given via the DSC 1 is comprehensive, yet not wanting further tightening of the rules, may sound contradictory. However, at the AGHE a vet or meat inspector will examine carcasses as they are processed. The trained hunter is really acting as a spotter, where anything that looks unusual is presented to qualified personnel for further examination before it enters the retail food chain.

Traceability

As noted, hygiene and traceability regulations need to be followed when a stalker is registered as a food business operator. It's not difficult, and mostly all that is needed is a common sense approach. The regulations about traceability (Articles 14 and 19 of Regulation 178/2002, and Regulation 931/2011) sound rather officious, but in practice, all that needs to be done is to record the supplier and destination of the product, using the one step forwards, one step back principle. This is carried out at each step up to the point of sale.

A stalker will not have a supplier, as he or she obtains from the wild, so they just need to record in the game book to whom they supply carcasses, with the date and amount, keeping any receipts obtained. Most stalkers will already do this for their cull records and estate accounts. The game tag is filled out by the stalker, so the dealer can fulfil his part of one step back, in having a record of the supplier, the amount, date and nature of the product supplied. This will help in tracing meat back to an unhygienic or illegal source, if necessary.

HACCP

Hazard Analysis Critical Control Point (HACCP) is a recognized system for food businesses to carry out a risk assessment of their food operation. It splits potential hazards into three categories, physical, microbiological and chemical, then looks at controls that can be put in place to manage or eliminate these risks. There are templates that can be downloaded, such as MyHACCP, from the Food Standards Agency, for example. This is comprehensive, but if the stalker needs to comply with 852/2004 in order to sell even small quantities of game meat, this will have to be carried out.

Many stalkers baulk at the paperwork and systems required, preferring to supply in-the-fur carcasses and/or give away venison for home consumption, which doesn't require this.

PRACTICALITIES

Hygiene and Temperature Requirements

Annex 1 of Regulation 852/2004 sets out the general hygiene requirements of primary production, including hunting and the handling and storage of game. For deer stalkers, this encompasses the chiller, vehicle and associated operations, including the evisceration at the premises to produce an in-the-fur carcass for later transportation to a dealer.

When I was employed as a meat inspector, the hygiene inspections of abattoirs and cutting rooms was done on a common-sense basis. We all know, surely, what clean and hygienic means; it's not rocket science. In our context, after a batch of deer has moved through a chiller, be it three or thirty, depending on size, all hair and debris is removed, the premises, hooks and gambrels are washed down with potable water and some mild disinfectant, then aired. Operations can then start again.

If I have six carcasses in my fridge, I will often go to the dealer with them during the day, clean the fridge and stalk the same evening, putting any shot deer back in. This would not have been a wasted job at all, as a cleaning cycle has been carried out, keeping the bacterial count low. The same happens at abattoirs country wide when operations stop at breakfast and lunchtime; debris is removed, followed by a good wash through with a hose or pressure washer, then

work re-commences; a deep clean is then carried out at the end of the day.

The vehicle transporting carcasses needs to be suitable, too. I use a watertight, high-sided fitted tray in my vehicle, easily removable and cleaned, to transport carcasses to my dealer 9 miles away. They sit on a raised grid, which allows any blood to drain below, keeping the carcass clean and dry. During this time the carcass temperature will not climb much before delivery to the dealer's chiller twenty minutes later. But others may have a much longer journey, and in this case either the stalker or estate will need a vehicle with a chiller, or if not economic, the dealer can pick up with his own temperature-controlled van. The time of year will also dictate how this is done, as even a reasonably short journey in the summer months may see carcass temperatures rise to unacceptable levels, which will break the cold chain requirement of maintaining less than 7°C throughout, although I maintain my fridge at a colder 4°C.

If a HACCP system is needed, the above will need to be recorded, temperatures taken regularly, and a cleaning schedule written up, adhered to and regularly reviewed.

Fridge and Cutting-Room Design

Looking at the layout of a larder facility, its general requirements are also covered in *The*

A fridge is essential for any serious stalker.

A carcass carrier: waterproof, with a grid to separate any blood dripping from the animal, and easy to remove and clean.

Wild Game Guide, although it is usually dictated by the space available. In an ideal scenario the carcass would come in at one end of a facility, the 'dirty' area, where it may have the green and/or red offal (pluck) removed, then pass into the fridge to cool, and out at a later date for transport to the dealer. Proper separation of waste such as green offal needs to be considered. For example I separate, bag and freeze any stomach and intestines I have after evisceration, instead of keeping it in the bottom of the deer fridge, to be disposed of later.

The chiller has to be of a suitable size for the throughput – a fridge designed for six deer will not adequately chill and ventilate the carcasses if ten warm sika are jammed inside. The building housing the chiller should have a secure roof with no falling debris such as bird droppings, it should be vermin proof, have good lighting, and available hot and cold potable water; it should also have a smooth concrete floor gently sloping to a central gully with a debris trap integral to the drain. Such a set-up would have the features of an ideal premises where venison carcasses could be kept for later transport to a dealer.

In addition to this, for home consumption the carcass can be skinned and then pushed along a rail to a 'clean' area where it can be cut into joints, as in the diagram attached. Packaged venison would leave by another door to avoid cross contamination, especially if there were carcasses entering while butchery was being carried out.

The Wild Game Guide says the operator handling game and game meat needs to be in good health, and to have undergone training in health risks. This person also needs to be aware of, and prevent the spread of, contagious diseases transmissible to humans, reporting any suspicions to the relevant authorities. This covers the hunter using a game facility as a staging post for in-the-skin carcasses to be delivered to an AGHE, and also a common-sense approach to producing venison meat for home consumption.

Larder layout for minimal cross contamination

An ideal small larder layout.

Disposal and Animal By-Products

Only about 35 per cent of a live deer is meat, roughly, so there is a fair amount of wastage that needs to be properly disposed of. The stalker can come across two types of animal by-products (ABP):

- That which is fit for human consumption but has no commercial value, or is not intended for use on aesthetic grounds, such as intestines, lungs or feet.
- By-products that are suspected of coming from a deer having a notifiable disease, such as tuberculosis or foot and mouth, for example, and which is covered by the ABP 2013 Regulations.

At the larder, bones, hide and unused meat is bagged and frozen, either to be taken to a refuse centre, or to be incinerated. A deep pit, dug at least 20m away from watercourses, can be very useful as a disposal area for the red and green offal, heads and feet. It must have at least 1m of soil to cap it, so it is best dug by machine and kept for use multiple times with a suitable covering. In the field and on the Scottish hill, green offal is often left for wildlife to eat, covered or partly buried and away from the general public. As this can include birds of prey, care must be taken to ensure there is no lead in anything that is left – another reason for the increasing use of lead-free bullets (*see* Chapter 5).

If the by-products and carcass are suspected of having a notifiable disease, ALHA need to be informed, and will give direction (*see* Chapter 9). If the stalker is left with the carcass and organs, these cannot be buried, and must be disposed of either by rendering in an approved premises, or by complete incineration in an approved incinerator.

Processing Unlimited Amounts of Venison for Wholesale or Retail

The Wild Game Guide sets out further criteria for the processing of game that will eventually be sold or, as the guide puts it, hygiene requirements for food business operators beyond primary production. In this scenario, probably not applicable to most stalkers, the hunter sells venison to wholesalers and/or the final consumer from a retail premises in unlimited quantities. This will require registration as an AGHE under veterinary control, licensed by the Foods Standards Agency in England and Wales, Foods Standards Scotland, or the Department of Agriculture and Rural Development (DARD) if located in Northern Ireland.

This came fully into force around 2010 and became too expensive for the small game dealer, as they had to factor in a full-time veterinary presence to oversee the operation. This resulted in the closure of many small game businesses, for having a vet on site sucked out any profit the

A premises for preparing larger quantities of venison for sale needs licensing by the FSA, and a full-time veterinary presence.

business made. Before the vet became necessary, a meat inspector would make regular visits to the various sites, at a much lower cost to the dealer. I don't see that a veterinary presence has made a marked improvement in public safety, but it had to be done to fall in line with EU practices, ensuring continued cross-border trade.

SUMMARY

As outlined above, there are many different scenarios that require working through in order to be sure that one is the right side of the law. In offering some general advice before converting or constructing a premises, a good way forward would be to make contact with one's Environmental Health officer with a proposed plan, and ask for their input. It would be free, and costly mistakes could be avoided by taking this route.

Whether Regulation 852/2004, 853/2004, 178/2002, the Food Safety Act 1990, or a combination of them needs to be followed, a well planned premises and chiller, sensible handling of warm carcasses, and subsequent delivery of cold carcasses or game meat would cover all bases, and need not cost an extortionate amount of money. Becoming a trained hunter, if you are not already one, via one of the routes discussed, ensures that the boxes are ticked for all eventualities that a part-time stalker might face.

FOOT AND MOUTH DISEASE

Foot and mouth is an acute viral disease affecting all cloven-hoofed animals, including deer. Although endemic in some parts of the world, the last two uncontained outbreaks in the UK were in 1967 and 2001. The 1967 outbreak was confined to a relatively small area of Northumberland, while the 2001 outbreak was countrywide. Personally, and as one heavily involved in that latter cull programme, I believe the extensive transportation of livestock around the country for slaughter in large abattoirs aided the spread of the 2001 outbreak. The initial infection was found to be on a farm in Northumberland, detected in pigs sent probably via Buckinghamshire to an abattoir in Essex. Historically, animals travelled only short distances to small, local slaughterhouses, but most of these ceased trading in the 1990s due to extensive and expensive red tape. Quite ironic really – unnecessary paperwork and legislation intended to improve red meat production ultimately aided the spread of a disease that caused tens of thousands of animals to be slaughtered.

The disease is spread rapidly; the clinical signs are of lethargy, loss of appetite and condition. Salivation and reluctance to walk are dependent on the severity of vesicles (blisters) around the mouth and dental pad, and around the top of and between the cleaves of the feet. It takes up to a week for exposed deer to show these signs. There is little danger of human infection to the stalker, for the virus crosses the species barrier with difficulty and with minor effect.

Once suspected in deer, APHA must be informed; meanwhile the carcass should be isolated and remain where found until the vet decides otherwise. Domesticated animal outbreaks are more likely, and the hunter will be aware of these via the national news.

TUBERCULOSIS

There are four types of tuberculosis (TB); the two that do not concern us as hunters are the human and fish types. As bovine TB affects humans, cattle, pigs and deer, cross infection from animal to human is important, thus making

Foot and mouth is a highly contagious disease among domesticated animals and deer.

Foot and mouth vesicle in a sheep's mouth, circled.

the disease notifiable. The two main routes of infection are by respiration – the deer inhaling the bacilli – and by ingestion, which can determine the site of lesions. Respiratory infection affects the lungs initially, and can spread to the inner surface of the ribcage. It is not unusual to find lesions far from this site, perhaps in lymph nodes in the haunch.

If infected by ingestion, the mesenteric lymph nodes will have one or a series of pus-filled abscesses, ranging in consistency from creamy to a hard, cheesy-like substance if long established. The three pairs of lymph nodes of the head can also be infected from either route of infection, the retropharyngeals mainly, but also the sub maxillaries and parotids. I always check the three sets. If head shot, one set may be unidentifiable, but usually there is something to incise.

If a TB-like lesion is found, a sample needs to be sent to APHA, who will give instruction about collection or delivery. In some parts of the country (at the time of writing), APHA are not collecting and testing, but are concentrating on known hotspots instead. However, it is one's responsibility to inform the authorities: what they then do is beyond the stalker's control.

If just one lesion is found, and nothing else in any of the viscera or lymph nodes throughout the body, the infection is localized and the carcass can pass into the food chain. Further lesions indicate a systemic spread and the carcass should be condemned.

To complicate things, it is hard to differentiate between avian TB, which is not transmissible to us, and the bovine type. A laboratory test is the only way to discover this. Localized avian TB

in deer shows as lower grade infections in the mesenteric and retropharangeal lymph nodes; however, these rarely become caseated and do not show the tubercle-like formations, so just the affected nodes need to be rejected.

RABIES

Rabies is a notifiable disease, but has been eradicated in the UK; the last human case caught from

Tuberculosis in fallow retros.

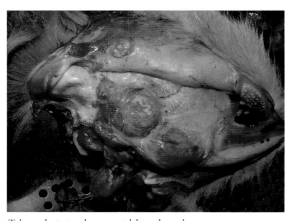
Tuberculosis in the parotid lymph node.

Tuberculosis in the mesenteric of a young fallow buck.

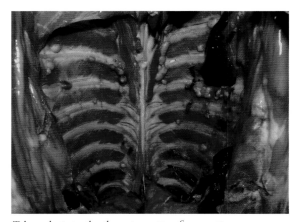
Tuberculosis in the thoracic cavity of a muntjac.

Hypoderma diana: *deer warble-fly larvae.*

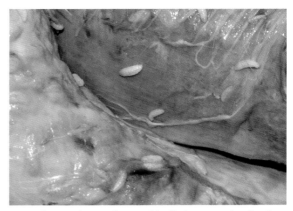

Hypoderma diana: *deer warble-fly larvae under the skin.*

animals other than bats was in 1902. However, rabies exists across Asia and Africa, and it is possible for the virus to the re-enter the UK through illegally imported animals from Europe, where it has been recorded in deer. The usual vector for humans is the dog.

Signs include salivation and foaming at the mouth, uncoordinated gait, aggressive behaviour, sexual excitement, paralysis and then death. Post mortem there are no visible signs as the virus affects the nervous system; changes in the brain substance by microscopical examination can confirm the disease.

WARBLE FLY

Usually associated with cattle, the warble fly affects deer also, although with a different variety of the *Hypoderma* fly: *H. bovis* and *H. lineateum* in cattle, *H. diana* in deer. Horses are accidental hosts also, but the larvae do not usually complete development.

The warble larvae are found under the skin of the affected deer, close to the spine. They can therefore spoil, though in visual terms only, the saddle or 'sirloin', in that extensive trimming may be necessary to make it presentable for human consumption. There is no adverse effect to human health, although in Scotland, since April 2015, the presence is notifiable to the local APHA.

The warble larvae emerge through the skin in spring, and drop to the ground where they pupate. In May/June the adult fly emerges, laying eggs on deer, which hatch and burrow under the skin, emerging the following spring to complete the cycle. The warble larvae cause distress to the deer, but the carcass is not unfit, and trimming is all that is necessary unless other side effects show, such as poorness due to irritation.

GENERAL CONDITIONS

ABOMASAL AND INTESTINAL ULCERATION

Abomasal and intestinal ulceration is often a symptom of winter death syndrome and stress. Post mortem the deer is seen to have ulcers in the abomasum (the last 'stomach' before the small intestine) and intestines, and these have perforated, resulting in peritonitis – inflammation of the lining of the abdominal cavity. Of course, winter death syndrome has its roots in malnutrition and extremely harsh weather conditions, so ulceration and peritonitis may be just one part of a greater problem. In 2018 a particularly hard, late winter in Scotland led to many deer deaths because the deer had used up the last of their fat reserves before spring arrived. No doubt these unfortunate animals would have had these symptoms had they been examined.

This condition results in total rejection of the carcass.

ACTINOMYCOSIS

Actinomycosis is a disease mainly of cattle, but deer can also be affected. It is an osteomylitis, affecting the bones of the lower jaw, and very occasionally the upper jaw also. The bone is thickened, enlarged, and in cross section reveals a honeycombed appearance, showing abscesses and suppurative areas. The abscesses may open internally to the mouth or externally to the skin of the jaw. The lymph nodes around this area do not have lesions, but may be enlarged.

Affected parts are rejected, but the disease, if advanced, may cause the condition of the animal to deteriorate to such an extent that poorness

Blackleg: a section of muscle.

and emaciation may lead to general rejection. *See also* the image on page 133, of the white-tailed deer with probable actinomycosis.

BLACKLEG OR BLACKQUARTER

Blackleg is another disease mainly of cattle, but sheep may also be affected, and occasionally deer. This is a soil-borne infective disease caused by the bacterium *Clostridium chauvoei*. Animals at pasture are mostly affected, however deer may feed on, or pass through, the infected pasture. It affects mainly young animals in good condition, and is usually fatal. The lesion is a swelling that crepitates (crackles) under pressure; it occurs mainly in the large muscles of the fore- or hindquarters, but may be found around the head and tongue. At post mortem, connective tissue is filled with a yellow, gelatinous liquid that oozes and is gassy. Lymph nodes are enlarged, muscle is black-red, and the carcass has a strong smell of rancid cheese or butter.

The carcass will be totally rejected.

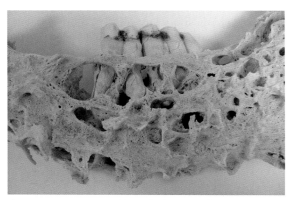
Actinomycosis in a jaw. Note the honeycombing, which in the live animal would be filled with suppurative material.

CONTAMINATION, INTERNAL

Internal contamination is not a condition as such, but its presence has a bearing on whether the

Actinomycosis in a live bovine.

Internal contamination due to poor shot placement.

CONTAMINATION, EXTERNAL

Deer recovery sometimes means dragging the carcass through the mud or over a livestock pasture, littered with dung. If it is apparent after the shot that recovery will be messy, sticking and evisceration should be delayed until a suitable area is found, or until back at the larder if this is within an hour. A drag mat or sled used at these times will aid hygienic extraction immeasurably. Thick mud ingrained in the hair will not be removed by washing; lesser wet contamination may be. The carcass is hung by the back legs, stuck and allowed to drain and dry externally. The carcass will need to be eviscerated carefully to avoid contaminating cut surfaces.

FAT NECROSIS

Fat necrosis shows as white, opaque areas of fat, amongst the normal, more yellow fat in the abdominal cavity. This is possibly due to a leakage of pancreatic juice from the pancreas, which acts on the fat, causing lesions.

Only local trimming is necessary.

HYPERTROPHY

Hypertrophy is an increase in the size of an organ. It is classically seen in a kidney: when one is functionally deficient, the other increases in size to compensate. A kidney that is four or five

carcass is fit for human consumption. A gut shot or a poorly eviscerated deer will have the whole of the abdominal cavity coated with gut content, intermixed with blood and faeces. A raking shot (one not taken at 90 degrees to the deer) can also carry that same mix into the pleural cavity. The carcass should be eviscerated while suspended by its back legs so all internal organs and liquid will drop down and away. Assuming there is no disease, limited parts of the carcass can be harvested.

Each case is different, but once carefully eviscerated and gently washed internally with a little water, the carcass is left to set, away from other uncontaminated carcasses. It is carefully skinned, still hanging up, keeping all knives clean throughout. The sirloins (backstraps) can be removed while in situ, the carcass sawn through at the pelvis and the two legs saved, as long as there is no visible gut content on the surfaces of the meat. All else is rejected.

Fat necrosis around kidney fat.

Kidney hypertrophy and infarcts; the other kidney is unaffected.

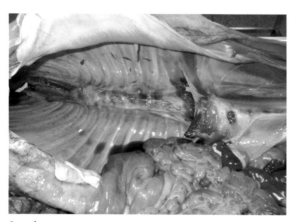

Jaundice.

times the size of the other can occur. Although fairly unusual, it has no bearing on the fitness of the carcass if the function of the organ is normal.

The affected part will be rejected.

INAPPETENCE

Not a condition or disease, inappetence often describes deer behaviour at the onset of winter. Possibly because they need to conserve energy for the hard months ahead as the days get short, deer move less and also eat less. Anecdotally, deer sightings are reduced until daylight hours

start to increase, well after the winter solstice around 21 or 22 December.

IMPERFECT BLEEDING

For the stalker, imperfect bleeding can occur in two instances. If the deer is head or neck shot then not subsequently stuck (bled out) within, say, an hour, blood can be retained in the muscle, liver, lungs and kidneys. When cut, blood runs out; the muscle is dark and has capillary bleeding. The other situation where the stalker may come across this is in attending road traffic accidents. The deer by the roadside may be nearly dead or dying (moribund) and/or highly stressed. Once killed, the animal will not bleed out. In both cases the carcass will not be passed as fit as the carcass does not set well, the muscle retaining much blood, which oozes when cut.

JAUNDICE (ICTERUS)

Jaundice is seen as a yellow colour change in the white tissues of the body – tendon sheaths, the whites of the eyes, bone cartilage, and fat most obviously. It is caused by bile pigments that have been absorbed into the bloodstream through cirrhosis of the liver and/or the blockage of bile ducts by parasites. The condition can be hidden somewhat by artificial light in a commercial premises, but the stalker, mostly working outside, will not be hindered. Jaundiced carcasses and offals are rejected.

There is also a condition caused by certain individual animals' inability to breakdown xanthophylls, which are pigments in grass. This pigment is deposited in the body and can be confused with jaundice. A simple laboratory test can differentiate the two; if the result shows that the colour is due to xanthophylls, the carcass is fit.

JOHNE'S DISEASE AND CHRONIC WASTING DISEASE (CWD)

Johne's disease and CWD are two quite distinct conditions, but to the hunter, whether observing a live deer through binoculars or when first

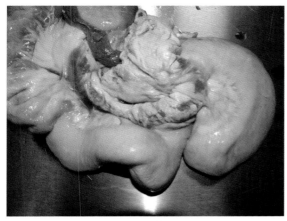

Johne's disease: enlarged areas of intestine.

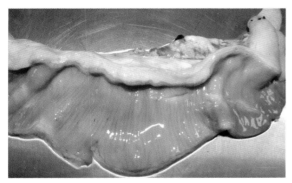

Johne's disease, showing a sectioned area of intestine and classic corrugations.

approaching a dead deer, the symptoms are the same: the body is very malnourished or underweight. Any deer showing these signs need to be assessed with caution. There is no personal danger, but if the animal is alive, its gait and behaviour may help to identify its condition.

CWD is a disease of the brain. Present for some fifty years in North America and three Canadian provinces, it has recently been detected in Norway and Finland. Fears that it may cross the North Sea mean that stalkers should be aware of this prion disease. (A prion is a type of protein that can cause normal proteins in the brain to fold abnormally, causing memory disfunction, personality changes and altered movements. Scrapie is another prion disease, discussed later in this chapter.) It may cause listlessness, a drooping head, perhaps the animal may be wandering

alone, unsteadily and/or in a repetitive pattern. It may drool and grind its teeth. These symptoms will obviously be lost upon the shot, so it is important to watch and note beforehand.

When opening the carcass, CWD will not present any noticeable conditions, but Johne's disease will. The classic symptom is a thickening of the intestinal wall, with white corrugations. There may be a fair amount of fat, which will be dead white, wet and sloppy, while the muscle will be wasted. The carcass may not set (that is, achieve rigor mortis) after hanging for twenty-four hours.

The carcass will be rejected in both cases.

MALIGNANT CATARRH FEVER

This is a fatal disease caused by a virus that is carried by sheep, but which does not affect them. In farmed deer the symptoms manifest themselves very quickly, with deer often dying within twenty-four hours of developing the fever. It is characterized by acute mucal discharge from the nose and eyes, often developing blindness. Diarrhoea is often seen.

The carcass will be totally rejected..

MASTITIS

Mastitis describes a septic inflammation of the udder. The organ can become septic for a variety of reasons, but post mortem the area is red, inflamed and hard to the touch. It exudes a fluid tinged with blood. Although the udder is normally removed from the carcass during evisceration, the associated lymph nodes may remain, being enlarged and watery if the condition is of long standing. Septic areas may develop, which lead to gangrene.

If localized, reject the udder and the underlying lymph nodes. If there is any evidence of further spread, reject the carcass.

MELANOSIS

Melanosis is a condition where the black pigment melanin is deposited in abnormal places around

Melanosis in the muscle between ribs.

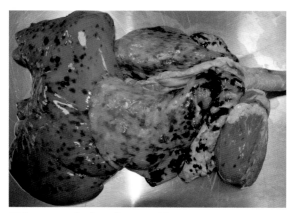

Melanosis in the liver, lungs and heart.

the body; normally it colours the hair, eyes and so on. Likely to be congenital, the pigment is deposited while still in the womb. When found, it can look like splashes of Indian ink and is strikingly obvious.

Steatosis.

Depending on the severity, affected parts are trimmed and rejected.

METRITIS

Metritis is a term for inflammation of the uterus, which alone is cause to reject the organ only. It can happen as a result of a rupture of the uterine wall during birth. However, this inflammation may occur with a retained placenta or foetus, which for whatever reason was not expelled on death and is obvious in a post-mortem examination. The foetus could be mummified if the condition is historic.

In a septic metritis the organ is much larger than normal, and contains a particularly foul-smelling brown or grey fluid. The vulva is swollen and has a discharge also. If it is necessary to look further, the associated lymph nodes will be greatly enlarged and congested. Usually the animal will be extremely ill if found live, and may not rise when approached. Left alone, it will rarely live for more than three or four days. Having worked for years in various abattoirs, I can attest that this condition is by far the worst smell I or my peers have encountered: it is truly gut turning.

The carcass will be totally rejected.

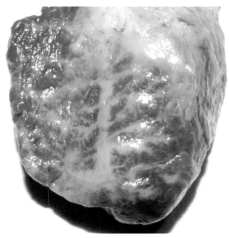

Muscular steatosis.

MUSCULAR STEATOSIS

Steatosis is described as a fatty change in an organ; muscular steatosis may be due to vascular restriction, muscle damage or denervation, but muscle is replaced with fat, with no reduction in the muscle bulk. Affected venison, being a lean meat, may have the look of well marbled beef, but restricted to a single muscle or muscle group; it is not noticeable until butchered.

The affected parts are rejected.

OEDEMA (DROPSY)

Oedema, or dropsy, is an excessive accumulation of clear fluid in cavities of the body. It can be associated with emaciation and conditions causing it (*see* below). Areas affected are the plural cavity (around the lungs), called a hydrothorax; ascites is the term for fluid in the peritoneal cavity containing the liver, intestines and stomach; and hydropericardium is fluid in the sac containing the heart. Anascara is fluid under the skin in subcutaneous tissue. Local oedema may be due to the obstruction of a vein or around an inflamed area, and may be trimmed if the cause is obvious.

Generalized oedema is usually a symptom of further health issues such as Johne's disease, TB, or heavy parasite infestations, and these carcasses are rejected.

POORNESS AND EMACIATION

The stalker should be aware of the distinction between the two, although the difference is often difficult to judge. In deer specifically, poorness can occur due to lack of food in the latter part of winter, causing 'winter death syndrome'. If the deer is shot, post mortem it will set well (rigor mortis will occur), and the fat, such as there is, will be normal in consistency. The muscle will be firm, dry and dark. The carcass is fit, but the meat will be tough so is often used for sausages or processing.

Emaciation, in comparison, is due to some pathological condition, a result of which is muscle wasting and a reduction of fat. However, the fat will be wet and soft, and gelatinous in severe cases. The muscle is soft, wet and flabby. Most tellingly, the carcass does not set after twenty-four hours of hanging, but remains wet

American white-tailed deer, with probable actinomycosis. Note the visible ribs and sunken haunches near the tail. It is in emaciated condition due to the diseased jaw.

Two abscesses here, and one in the head – the carcass was rejected.

A road traffic accident: this deer crawled some 400m on broken and exposed knee bones.

or gets even wetter. The carcass will be totally rejected.

PYAEMIA

Pyaemia is a condition in which a local infection has not been contained by the lymph nodes; bacteria is then carried around the body by the blood, and lodges in the lungs, kidneys and liver, possibly elsewhere, causing secondary abscesses. In general terms, a single site of infection or abscess is trimmed, but if a second or third site is found, total rejection of the carcass is warranted. *See* septic arthritis and tick pyaemia as examples, below.

ROAD TRAFFIC ACCIDENTS (RTAs)

Many deer are injured each year by collision with vehicles. They can travel many hundreds of metres to cover with multiple broken limbs and other bones, where they may then lie up. A slow death awaits, so any reports of RTAs should be followed up with a wide search. The accompanying image shows a fallow 400m from a road with both front legs broken, bones visible. The animal was found alive, but had a terrible smell, due to pyaemia.

SCRAPIE

Scrapie is a disease in sheep and goats, but it has been shown that it can be transmitted to deer (US Department of Agriculture[3]). It is spread through colostrum and milk, also from infected pastures where animals have given birth and deer may later graze. Affecting the central nervous system, it is detected in the live animal through behavioural changes, including biting the legs, flanks and belly due to itchiness, grinding the teeth, rubbing the body against a static object (hence 'scrapie'), a wild eye look, and charging fences and dogs. In advanced cases, the gait will be uncoordinated and the animal will have a tendency to fall. However, no gross lesions will be present in the carcass. The sheep or goat with this prion disease (*see* brief prion explanation under CWD) will be readily noticed by the farmer; however, in the wild the milder symptoms will go undetected.

Domesticated animals identified with scrapie will be condemned.

SEPTICAEMIA

When bacteria gain a foothold in the blood and multiply, a septicaemia is indicated. Classically shown in anthrax, but otherwise an animal will be extremely ill; the carcass will show as highly fevered, with much blood retained in the spleen and tissues. Petechial haemorrhages, looking like a rash, may be present throughout the tissues of the kidneys, heart, lungs and intestine. The liver may be swollen and cloudy. Total rejection and possible notification to the local veterinary office is indicated, as this could be the initial onset of anthrax – although animals with this disease die quickly, so this stage of anthrax is brief.

SEPTIC ARTHRITIS

Arthritis may affect the knee and hock joints of a deer without having an impact on the fitness of the carcass to join the food chain. If the arthritis becomes septic, care must be taken to ensure that the bacteria have not become systemic: a pyaemia. If just one joint has pus in it, the leg is trimmed back, having checked the associated lymph nodes. If further abscesses are found, the carcass is rejected.

TICK PYAEMIA

Although tick pyaemia is a well documented disease in lambs, deer are also hosts and can be affected. This disease is transmitted mainly via the common sheep tick *Ixodes ricinus* (there are also five others), which pass the bacteria to young lambs while feeding on their blood. Being immature, the body's immune system cannot cope, and abscesses develop in various parts of the body. The symptoms are a reluctance to move, inappetence, lameness, paralysis of the rear end if abscesses affect the spinal cord, and ultimately

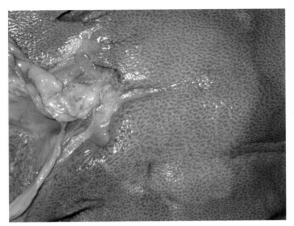

Septicaemia shown in the liver as petechial haemorrhages.

Septic arthritis in the knee joint.

death. If chronic (a lower level of infection, over the longer term) there may be lameness in one or more limbs with pus in the joints, muscle or tendons, with small abscesses in the lungs and liver; the animals are weak in development.

The carcass is unfit for human consumption.

Tick numbers are increasing due to a general

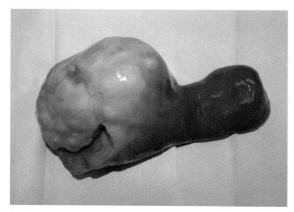

Kidney tumour.

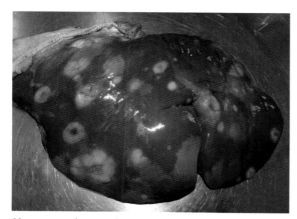

Hepatic neoplasia, or liver cancer.

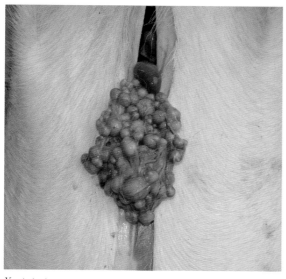

Yersiniosis.

rise in temperatures, probably through climate change, as the average temperature needs to be above 7°C or ticks remain dormant. Perhaps this may become a condition of increasing prevalence.

TUMOURS

There are two types of tumour: benign and malignant. Both are described as abnormal growths of new tissue, having no purposeful function; they may be found in most parts of the body.

Benign tumours: These are usually normal in appearance, being extensions of the parent tissue, and are localized. Examples are papilloma (warts), lipoma, tumours of the fat cells and fibromas, and tumours of the fibrous tissue cells. Affected parts are rejected.

Malignant tumours: This is abnormal tissue, having much growth energy, and lacking the restraint of normal tissue. The cells may invade normal tissue by direct or contiguous growth. They may infiltrate the lymph and blood vessels, where they break away and are carried to other body sites, a process called metastasis. When deposited, the cells multiply, a characteristic feature of the malignant tumour. Carcinomas are generally spread by the lymph system and are a disease of middle or old age, whereas sarcomas, spread by the bloodstream, can occur at any age.

Single, localized tumours are either trimmed, or the affected organ is rejected. Carcasses with numerous tumours are rejected.

YERSINIOSIS

Yersiniosis is a disease of mainly young, farmed deer, caused by *Yersinia pseudotuberculosis*. Symptoms in live deer are a sudden loss of condition with watery, smelly diarrhoea. Death can be quick. Post mortem, lesions are confined to the intestine, which will be oedematous and haemorragic; the associated lymph nodes will be enlarged, watery and necrotic.

The carcass will be totally rejected; there is no danger to the stalker.

CONDITIONS OF SPECIFIC PARTS

HEART

The heart may not always be in a fit state for the hunter to inspect, as many deer are shot in this area (heart/lung shot). There are a few conditions that one may look for in this organ, although none are, on their own, cause for complete rejection.

Epicarditis and Pericarditis

Epicarditis and pericarditis are terms for the inflammation of the surface of the heart muscle, the epicardium and pericardium (the sac containing the heart), respectively. In acute cases of septicaemia the pericardium is roughened on the exterior and a brown/grey colour. This may also be due to an infection in the lungs or pleura cavity.

The heart is rejected if the condition is localized, but it often indicates a more serious systemic infection elsewhere, so total rejection is often warranted.

Cysticercus ovis Cysts

These cysts are unusual in the deer heart, but have been reported. *C. ovis* is the cystic stage of the dog tapeworm *Taenia ovis*. It is seen as an opaque white, hard cyst in the heart muscle, about 5–8mm in diameter. There is no risk to

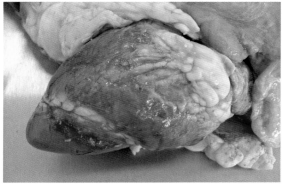

Epicarditis, showing inflammation of the surface of the heart muscle. To the right the pericardium can be seen, thickened and dark with pus. This indicates a septicaemia.

humans, as the tapeworm is specific to the dog and fox.

The heart alone is rejected if a single cyst is found, and no further cysts in the diaphragm or intercostals (muscle between the ribs), both being sites of prevalence. However, if two or more cysts are found in the heart or elsewhere, the carcass is rejected as, short of slicing the whole thing into small pieces, one could find more cysts virtually anywhere.

LIVER

The liver is the largest internal organ with a huge blood supply, and is therefore important in meat inspection. Many conditions are transported

C. ovis: *a viable cyst in the heart showing the scolex inside (circled).*

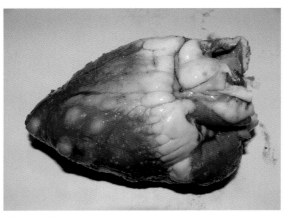

Multiple C. ovis *cysts in the heart; these are not viable.*

around the body in the blood so are liable to affect the liver, as pathogens pass through, or are held in the liver substance. The following tenuicollis and hydatid cyst conditions are caused by intestinal tapeworms of the dog and fox, which affect deer in that they are the intermediate hosts. Hydatid cysts affect humans as we can also be intermediate hosts and develop cysts, so it is important in meat inspection.

Cysticercus tenuicollis

Cysticercus tenuicollis relates to the liver in that the migratory tracks of the dog tapeworm *Taenia hydatigena* embryos, en route from the intestine to the abdominal cavity, pass through the liver substance, leaving white, wiggly, thread-like lines, the 'tenuicollis tracks'. For the hunter, such livers may be found in deer that frequent public footpaths and areas where dogs are often walked. Dogs that are not regularly wormed will excrete the eggs, which are picked up by grazing deer, thus furthering the life cycle. (The cycle is as follows: dog intestinal worm > excretes eggs > eggs ingested by grazing deer > embryos hatch internally and become cysts > dog eats deer and cysts > worms hatch in the dog.)

If only one or two tracks are found, local trimming may save the liver; otherwise it is rejected.

The embryos often die when emerging from the liver, but should they make it to the next stage in life, they will form a cyst in the abdominal cavity. These are up to 7cm in diameter, watery in consistency, and hang on a long neck; they are not embedded in the viscera or tissues. They have just one scolex or 'egg' visible inside.

The cyst/cysts can be removed, the carcass is fit for consumption; there is no risk to humans as the cysts and intestinal worms are host specific.

Hydatid Cysts

Hydatid cysts are not known to be prevalent in deer, but as they can affect humans it is good to be aware of them. Their life cycle is as follows: dog or fox excretes ova, which are ingested by an intermediate host – this can be all domestic animals and man. The capsules dissolve in the intestine, and the embryos burrow through to the portal vein. Some then lodge in the liver, or can be carried in the bloodstream to the lungs, kidneys and spleen, but they can lodge elsewhere in the body. Cysts develop with a thick capsule, containing many daughter cysts, which can be seen floating inside. The cycle completes when a dog (or fox) eats the flesh or organ containing the cysts. Tapeworms then develop (*Echinoccus granulosus*), living in the intestine, and produce ova. The cysts are often embedded in tissue but can be attached with a 'neck'. They differ from the benign (to humans) *C. tenuicollis*, which are soft and watery to the touch, and contain only one scolex.

Much care should be taken to make sure that the viscera of an animal containing just one cyst

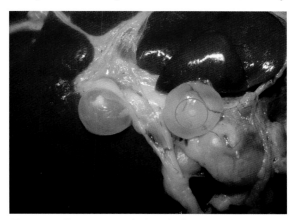

C. tenuicollis *cysts attached to the liver. A viable scolex is visible (circled).*

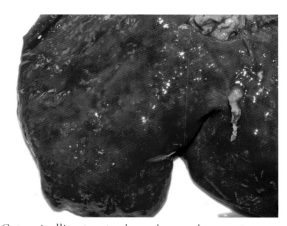

C. tenuicollis *migrating larvae have made serpentine tracking in the liver.*

is destroyed. A cyst is viable up to a week after the organ to which it is attached is discarded. Sterilization, or the immersion of a cut cyst in a saturated salt solution, will kill the scolexes. If, as a result of hydatid disease, the carcass is emaciated or oedematous, the carcass is condemned.

Humans live for a much longer period than all the animal species discussed here. If a person is unlucky enough to ingest an ova, it can grow to football-size proportions over a lifetime. I know a very senior meat inspector, also a countryman with many working gundogs, who would never let a dog lick his hand or face, unless he knew, without any doubt whatsoever, that it had been wormed within three months, the time needed to complete a lifecycle. He has seen too many hydatid cysts in his working life to risk harbouring the cysts himself.

Liver Fluke

Liver fluke are seen when incising the portal opening. The fluke (*Fasciolia hepatica*) are a dark brown-red, leaf-like in shape, and live in the bile ducts. They can cause cirrhosis and reduced liver function, which in rare cases may be fatal. Otherwise there are few indicating signs visually in the liver. If there are no other signs of poor condition, just the liver is rejected, and the rest of the carcass is judged fit for consumption. Sheep and cattle are more prone to fluke infestation, as the intermediate host, the snail, tends to deposit eggs on the lower part of grass stems, which deer usually do not browse, being light grazers and taking just the top of vegetation.

Hydatid cysts in an old cow's liver.

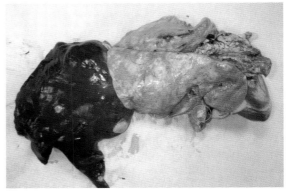

Hydatid cysts in a sheep's liver and also the lungs (circled).

Fasciola hepatica *in the liver. Deer do not get pipy ducts, as shown in this image of a sheep's liver (circled).*

Fasciola hepatica, *liver fluke.*

Umbilical Pyaemia

This is a condition affecting young deer. After birth, bacteria can enter the umbilical fissure and lodge in the liver (to which the umbilical cord was connected prior to birth), causing an abscess. Being young, resistance may not be sufficient to stop the spread of infection bodywide and a pyaemia may result, killing the animal. If found before death, the deer will be listless and extremely ill and should not enter the food chain.

Should the animal survive until adulthood, a heavily encased abscess may be found in the liver, indicating that the bacterial spread was arrested. Care must be taken to see if other abscesses are present anywhere else in the body. If not, the carcass is fit; if other abscess sites are found, the carcass is rejected.

Fatty Liver

This condition shows a liver that is a pale brown and dull on the surface, as opposed to being dark brown and shiny, which indicates a healthy liver. It is caused by two fairly obvious natural occurrences in deer: the rut in the male, and after birth in the female, both of which results in a negative energy balance. During the rut a buck or stag will be drawing on fat reserves rather than eating, and a doe or hind will be drawing on its reserves in producing enough milk for her young, in both

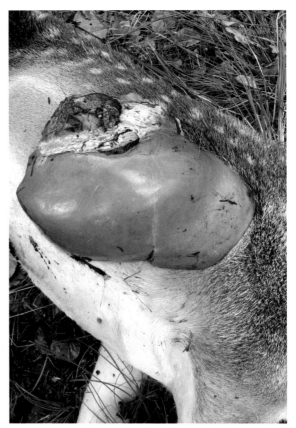

Fatty liver of a fallow buck, after the rut.

cases more fat than the liver can process, hence the buildup. The time of year indicates when the condition will occur – May/June in the female, broadly July/August for roe bucks, and October/November for other species, depending on local variations. If a doe is shot with such a liver it may be out of season. There is nothing intrinsically wrong with the liver in either case, but it is probably not the best eating. The liver will return to normal after the event has passed.

Reject the liver.

LUNGS

The lungs are a primary and secondary site of infection for many conditions. This may be firstly by inhalation, airborne tuberculosis bacteria being a good example. Also the very fine blood capillaries, where gaseous exchange between

An umbilical hernia; abscesses were found inside the carcass, which was rejected.

Pleurisy, on the inner surface of the ribs.

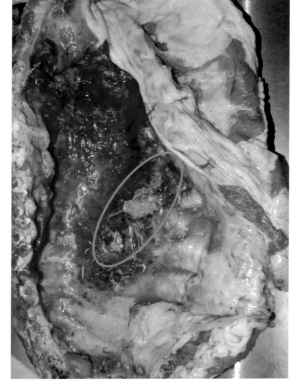

Septic pleurisy showing the red, fevered pleura and areas of pus (circled).

the bloodstream and atmosphere takes place, can trap bacteria liberated into the bloodstream from a primary site elsewhere in the body. This may take the form of abscesses and pleurisy, which is the adhesion of the lung to the inner surface of the ribcage.

This can arise for a variety of reasons, including mechanical damage to the ribs themselves, such as being trodden on by a larger deer, or by antler damage. Unless abscesses are present in the carcass, the plura is stripped away, and no further action is needed. However, septic pleurisy will bring down the animal's general condition, such that it will be necessary to condemn the carcass.

Lungworms

Lungworms have a fascinating life cycle. Very broadly, eggs are laid by the adult female in the air passages, and these are coughed up, swallowed, and passed out in the faeces. The larvae are then picked up either by the deer directly, or in some cases by an intermediate host, which is not itself infected. This may be a snail or slug: the larvae pass through it and are excreted. Larvae that are ingested by deer while grazing pass through the intestinal wall into the lymph and bloodstream to the lungs; here they are arrested by the tiny capillaries, and pass through to the air passages where they hatch into adults. Thus the cycle starts over again.

Affected lungs have slightly depressed areas that are somewhat brighter red in colour than the surrounding lung tissue. Alternatively lung tissue may be grey, and be of a solid nature when cut, as opposed to the spongy feel of the healthy lung.

Muellerius capillaris

These worms are often found in older animals in great numbers. They cause nodules about the

Muellerius capillaris *nodules in the lungs.*

Dictyocaulus viviparus *(circled) in the lung air passages.*

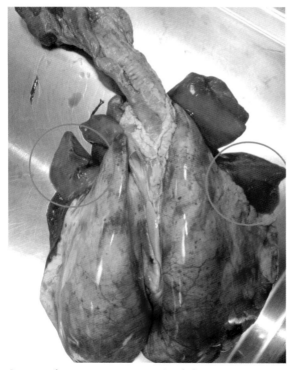

Lungs with enzootic pneumonia (circled).

size of no. 6 shot, and are reddish-brown or grey in colour; they are hard when palpated. Only the lungs need be rejected.

Dictyocaulus viviparus

These worms cause pneumonia and bronchitis, being found in the bronchioles or larger air passages of the lungs; they can be seen with the naked eye. Affected animals have a hoose-like cough, which is somewhat husky; the animal may extend its neck and tongue while doing so. The condition is often fatal. Only the lungs must be rejected.

Protostrongylus rufescens

Yellowish nodules in the lung substance, with no inflammation; the worm is not visible to the eye. Affected deer can 'bark'. The condition may cause serious losses. In the carcass only the lungs are rejected.

Elaphostrongylus cervi

Nodules are scattered throughout the lung, so the lung is rejected.

Pneumonia

Pneumonia is fluid in the air sacs (alveoli), often caused by lungworms. It shows whitish areas near the edges of the lung tissue, often with a raised surface. The tissue when cut is firm and solid, as opposed to the light, spongy feel of a healthy lung. This can become septic, causing pus to be present. Pneumonia is often associated with pleurisy (*see* above). Enzootic pneumonia will cause areas of the lungs to be dark pink, heavy and filled with fluid. If a piece is cut and placed in water it will not float, as opposed to healthy lung tissue, which will.

Unless other ills are present only the lungs are rejected.

Echinococcus or Hydatid Cysts

See liver section for details.

KIDNEYS

Kidneys are not often discussed with regard to deer. In the abattoir, all kidneys of domesticated animals are inspected by peeling their fibrous case away, visually inspecting them, and slipping them back into their casing again to stop them drying out. I always look at the kidneys of deer I have shot as they will give a full picture of the animal's condition.

Congenital Cysts and Kidney Stones

These two conditions are notable, but do not affect the fitness of the carcass in any way. Congenital cysts may be small, grain sized, and irregularly distributed throughout both kidneys.

The kidneys only are rejected.

Hydronephrosis

Hydronephrosis is a blockage in the ducts from the kidney, such that urine backs up and cannot be processed by the organ. The ducts to and from the kidney may be grossly enlarged, and the surrounding fat soggy. The carcass may have a distinct smell if both kidneys are affected, meaning that the carcass is unfit for consumption. If only one is blocked, the other may process enough urine that the carcass is fit, in which case local trimming may only be necessary if lightly affected.

Infarcts

Infarcts are small, local bacterial infections or blockages in the kidney pelvis, causing a wedge-shaped infarct, broadening at the outer kidney surface. The infarct is lighter in colour than the surrounding kidney tissue.

These are of little importance on their own, but the kidney should be rejected.

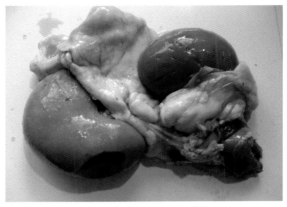

Hydronephrosis. The pale kidney on the left had urine backed up in the ducts.

Nephritis, showing a dull, pitted surface.

Nephritis

Nephritis is a catch-all term for anything abnormal in the kidney. The surface of the kidney is usually pitted, and the colour is dull and pale as opposed to the shiny brown of a healthy kidney. The condition may be caused by localized bacteria. If there are no other indications of ill health, the kidney/s is/are discarded.

Petechial Haemorrhages

These are small but very numerous haemorrhages throughout the kidney, which look like a rash; they indicate a fever probably brought on by a systemic infection or a septicaemia. If other areas are also affected, the carcass is rejected.

Petechial haemorrhages in kidney.

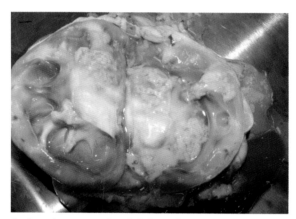

Pyelonephritis in a sheep's kidney, showing pus and tissue degeneration.

Deer keds.

Pyelonephritis

Pyelonephritis is an infection that usually starts in the bladder, then rises to the pelvis (core) of the kidney. It shows as a thick, slimy fluid with pus intermixed. Usually there is a strong smell of ammonia, and the area around the kidney/s may be glairy and inflamed. Normally the carcass is totally rejected, unless the kidney is very slightly affected.

SKIN

Deer Keds

Deer keds emerge from pupae on the ground, then fly up to take residence on deer, where they lose their wings and spend the rest of their lives. Keds are up to 7mm long, have six legs on a flat body and are brown in colour. They seem to cause little disturbance to deer. If they transfer to humans during evisceration or lardering, they can scurry about the head, moving quickly through hair and causing minor irritation but, as they do not burrow, little further issue arises.

Lice

Lice on deer are often a sign of poor general condition. In themselves they pose no risk to the deer or to humans, as they are quite host specific. Deer lice are small, some 1–2mm long, pale grey but reddish if full of blood from the host. The live eggs, nits, are a pale white.

Lice.

Lice live around the ears, moving to the groin when the thicker winter coat develops. Deer usually lose the infestation when the coat is shed, but an animal in poor condition holds the winter coat for longer, thus keeping the lice. This causes more irritation, which can lead to a further loss of condition – a downward spiral. A heavy lice infestation may indicate a poor animal, and careful inspection of the carcass is warranted before judgement is passed.

Nasal bot larvae.

Mud Fever

This is a dermatitis caused by external conditions. A wet, constantly muddy habitat may cause hair loss to the area just above the hooves, and the skin will become patchy and discoloured, perhaps with scabs that ooze liquid. However, this should not affect the fitness of the carcass.

Nasal Bot Fly

Nasal bots are the larvae of the nasal bot fly; the larvae or maggots grow up to 3cm (1.2in) in length in the nasal cavity and frontal sinuses of a deer, after being deposited by the fly at the nasal entrance. When mature, the larvae are sneezed out and deposited on the ground. The fly emerges and is active in the spring and late summer for only a few days, completing its cycle by depositing larvae at the nose of the deer. While deer may harbour the bots, they do no great harm, producing some discharge and causing a cough or sneezing. It is possible for humans to harbour them, although this is unusual.

Inspection-wise, the larvae are not important, but they may irritate the deer when alive.

Contagious Ecthyma

Contagious ecthyma is a highly infectious virus of mainly sheep and goats, affecting the muzzle, lips and udder, and occasionally occurring around the eyes and coronary band of the hooves. Commonly known as 'orf' – also contagious pustular dermatitis – infected older animals will recover, healing within a month. Dependent lambs and no doubt deer kids may die as they are unable to suckle due to lesions, becoming emaciated.

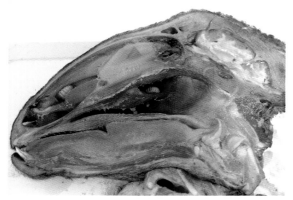

Sheep-nostril fly larvae in a sectioned head, similar to deer-nostril fly larvae.

Farm and abattoir workers, butchers and sheep shearers can be a source of transmission, also becoming infected with a papule, which develops into a small scab around a cut or abrasion in the skin. In uncomplicated cases it clears without scarring in three to six weeks. A low-grade fever may be present for a few days.

If the deer carcass is accompanied with inflammation of the intestine and stomach and/or pneumonia, it is condemned. Otherwise it is considered fit.

Ticks

Ticks are important to the hunter as they can carry and transmit Lyme disease by locking on, burrowing into the skin, and feeding on the blood of the host. Ticks are not host specific, so a tick may feed on three types of animal during its three-year life, which makes it an important vector in transmitting disease across species. Each of the three stages are similar in that the

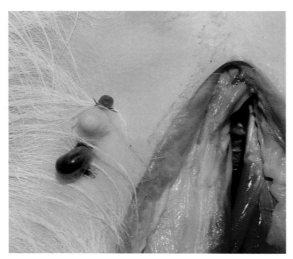

Embedded ticks on a deer carcass.

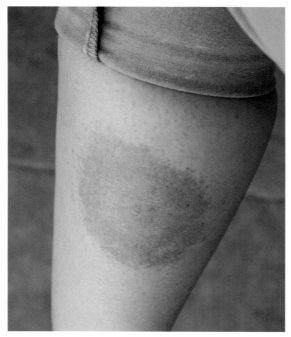

'Bull's-eye' rash on a human leg caused by tick infection. Not everyone will get this distinctive symptom of Lyme disease.

in colour, with six or eight legs, and are 8–10mm long. When engorged with blood, the females have a rounded, grey-brown body.

A heavy infestation of ticks is, in itself, no reason to reject the carcass, but a particularly heavy infestation and a poor carcass may need further investigation, and a search for other clinical signs.

Lyme disease: This is a serious and debilitating chronic disease in humans, characterized by a circular 'bull's-eye' red rash, appearing seven to thirty days after infection around the area of the tick bite. Typically this is around 15cm (6in) in diameter, but it can be larger or smaller. However, it is important to know that one in three people with Lyme disease will not develop the rash.

Initial symptoms include tiredness, muscle and/or joint pain, headaches, a high temperature and a stiff neck. Later, even after some months or years, swelling and pain in the joints can develop, along with numbness, paralysis of the facial muscles, memory issues and difficulty concentrating; also heart problems and inflammation around the brain – meningitis – causing severe headaches, a stiff neck, and sensitivity to light. Some people go on to develop chronic fatigue syndrome.

If any of these symptoms develop, a visit to the doctor and a blood test will be in order. Even after a negative test, another test may be needed if symptoms persist, as a negative result may not have identified the disease.

Prevention consists of impenetrable clothing, such as tucking trouser legs into socks. Some proprietary clothing includes a long-lasting repellent, which apparently works well.

Removing ticks found on the body within twenty-four hours is said to reduce the possibility of infection, using a tick removal tool as opposed to pinching with the fingers, which may leave the head buried in the skin.

tick drops off the host into undergrowth, reattaching the following year to gorge on blood for a week before dropping off again. The female can treble in size due to blood intake, while the smaller male stays the same size. Ticks are brown

Papillomata

Papillomata are warts, a tumour of skin cells; they are benign (localized and encapsulated). The cells show no great variation from those of normal tissue. Just affected parts are rejected.

Warble Fly

See 'Notifiable Diseases' section.

SPLEEN

The spleen, as part of the lymphatic system, can be enlarged when seen in anthrax and other septicaemias, and hydatid cysts may occasionally be present. In imperfectly bled carcasses the spleen will be engorged and dark.

STOMACH AND INTESTINES

Conditions affecting these organs are systemic rather than specific to the contents of the abdominal cavity only, so are covered elsewhere:

Abomasal and intestinal ulceration
Johne's disease
Parasites: tapeworms, hydatid cysts and *C. tenuicollis*
Tuberculosis
Yersiniosis

Chapter 10

Looking Ahead

There are many factors that will impact deer stalking in the next ten years. I have highlighted some here, but there will be others, too. If chronic wasting disease gains a hold in the UK deer population for example, the result would be as catastrophic to deer management as the Covid-19 pandemic on our economy and way of life in 2020.

INCREASING UK WOODLAND COVER

The UK has relatively little woodland cover compared to other European countries. This matters greatly, as climate change is such an important issue. Woodlands soak up and store a large amount of carbon dioxide, the gas that is largely responsible for global warming. We are all aware of the movement away from fossil fuels, but the ever-increasing human population and their rising standard of living means carbon emissions are hard to contain.

The UK, as a whole, has just 13 per cent woodland cover, split between England at 10 per cent, Scotland 18 per cent, Wales 15 per cent and Northern Ireland 8 per cent. Compare these figures to Germany with 33 per cent, France 31 per cent, Italy 31 per cent and Spain with 37 per cent woodland cover.[1] While a young wood can capture over 400 tonnes of carbon per hectare, it is estimated that to become carbon neutral by 2050, the UK needs to plant some 1.5 million hectares of additional woodland to help achieve this, an area the size of Yorkshire.[2] The government is committed to planting more woodland, taking the coverage for England to 12 per cent by 2060, but this is fraught with difficulties, and many interested parties such as the Forestry Commission, the Royal Forestry Society and the Woodland Trust do not think this is achievable. They cite issues with the convoluted grant system and difficulty in persuading private landowners to plant new areas of tree cover.

Whatever the problems, however much new woodland is actually planted, it will help restore our native species abundance (individuals within a species), of which we have lost some 13 per cent since the 1970s. This is good news for Britain's wildlife, of course, and to bring the subject round to deer, the new habitat is excellent news for them, too. For deer stalkers this could mean more land to shoot over, which on the face of it is good news. But will the deer population rise in line with more planted woodland?

TECHNOLOGY

I believe a big factor in this is, maybe surprisingly to the reader, the use of the thermal imager and digital technology. Technologically the digital rifle scope is rapidly advancing, taking over for use at night from the image-intensifying tubed devices, which work very effectively but are damaged by use in daylight. A digital scope is not, so it can be a permanent fixture to a rifle, usable in colour by day, and black and white or green at night, with appropriate infra-red illumination (light that is invisible to our own eyes and those of animals). I have no doubt that such scopes will develop further, with higher resolution processors and screens, becoming a viable alternative for the more traditional optical scope. Digital is especially useful at dawn and dusk without an illuminating torch, and the models I have tested gave better resolution at these times than the very best of the available optical scopes.

It is my opinion that we are at the start of a sea change in optics, which will play out during this decade. The thermal imaging rifle scope is with us too. I know it is used by some for deer stalking, but I don't see it as an acceptable tool for the average hunter, for it doesn't allow the species, age or any nuanced information of behaviour to be seen before the shot.

As discussed in Chapter 5, deer stalking has traditionally been a labour-intensive activity, with many hours spent in the field searching through binoculars for well camouflaged deer among the flora. The actual return for hours spent is hard to quantify, but it has been estimated that a lot of part-time stalkers have success on one out of four outings. This obviously does not cover ground where deer may be in abundance, but let us take that as a starting point. Those same hunters with a thermal imager can now spot any living creature within a kilometre of him or herself, if in plain sight. Walking through woods, a deer huddled up under a bush or against a bank would be plainly visible, whereas previously the stalker may well have walked on by, unaware of its presence. This has certainly been my own and my peers' experience, and it has transformed our stalking absolutely. Sometimes such deer spotted in undergrowth using a thermal device just cannot be seen through the optical scope mounted on a rifle, as it's too dark – but with a digital scope that will change, and the deer's advantage will again be reduced.

Wider evidence of the utility of thermal technology is found with the increase in deer carcasses brought to game dealers. My own dealer, one of the larger game businesses in the country, saw an increase in throughput in 2018/19, and larger still in 2019/20, when they stopped taking carcasses for a while over the winter, such were the numbers coming in. Other dealers have been similarly inundated with carcasses. The only change that has happened over those years is the availability of the imager, now half the price it was just four years previously. A basic model cost £2,000 then, whereas now it is around £900, meaning that this technology is available to many more hunters.

Perhaps the success rate of the part-time stalker has been raised to one in two outings using a thermal spotter, but it is clear that more deer than ever before are being culled. On the one hand this is good news, as the country's rising deer population has been well documented over recent years. Efforts to stop the increase,

Image through a digital scope in daylight; this technology is improving all the time.

keen on field sports, so this decline is predicted to accelerate.[4] In Europe, France, Italy, Germany and the Nordic countries are seeing a similar hunting demographic, which does not bode well for the future.

In opposition to this, here in the UK, firearms licence grants are rising, and strong competition for stalking ground has pushed up the cost of leases, as discussed in Chapter 5. Observers say the wide availability of courses to ease one's entry into deer stalking has attracted many into the activity. With basic introductory weekend courses, paid stalks with a professional guide and then perhaps buying into a syndicate, one's path is helped enormously. This has coincided with widespread reports of 'peak stuff' – that is, people have enough possessions and are now turning their attention to experiences to fill their leisure time. Deer stalking is accessible, so why not give it a try, being the thought. Perhaps this is sustainable, but many novice stalkers complete some sort of training only to be frustrated at the lack of reasonably priced stalking available to them. Maybe the numbers of UK stalkers will also decline over time, but for different reasons than in other countries.

VEGETARIANISM

The UK has a growing number of vegetarian and vegan adherents, currently estimated at some 8 per cent of the population. It is forecast that by 2025, some 25 per cent will be vegetarian (including vegans).[5] There is also a general rise in the so-called 'flexitarians', who consciously eat less meat or have two or three meat-free days per week.

Quite what this predicts is uncertain, but at the very least there seems to be a growing polarization between those hunting and presumably eating venison, and people refusing meat for various reasons. I don't wish to go into the vegetarian arguments: suffice to say they appeal on many different fronts – animal production of greenhouse gases, maximizing the use of land, and exploitation of the animals themselves, to name three. My point is that red meat production can be reduced to match this slowdown in demand, but venison, a product of wild animal

numbers being controlled, would not be so easy to manage and could create a permanent over-supply. This happened in early 2020: imports of farmed venison from New Zealand and, I'm told, Spain caused carcass prices to slump, down from £2.20/kg to £1.00/kg for fallow, for example. The excess imported venison coincided with larger domestic production, as noted above. Game dealers think these lower prices are here to stay.

The rest of Europe, our main export market, is slowly becoming less carnivorous as well, so in the longer term presumably less venison will be sold abroad also.[6]

To counteract this over-supply, the Wild Venison Working Group[7] has been formed, chaired by the Forestry Commission, which is looking at ways of increasing domestic consumption. I sincerely hope they succeed in doing so, but they are facing an increasingly informed population. The general public will, for example, watch David Attenborough's important *Extinction* documentary about man's unnecessary and cruel exploitation of white rhinos, pangolins and other animals for the Asian market and wrongly attribute those issues to our domestic deer population. We do not have an extinction problem with our deer (in fact we have the opposite at present), but it is not difficult to see how the vegetarian/vegan movement, exposés of illegal animal practices in other countries and a largely young, informed, urban population would coalesce these concerns, creating more of an aversion to eating the meat of wild animals shot in our countryside at the precise time we produce record amounts of venison. A perfect storm of media attention, social trends and changing eating habits!

In my own response to this, I have been exploring the practicalities of my game dealer cutting up and vacuum packing some of the carcasses I take to him. While I have a licensed premises, it is only an 'in the fur' storage facility. I cannot sell on venison I produce in larger amounts, but can give it away (as discussed in Chapter 8). By getting him to process the carcass, as a well-regulated AGHE, I would be allowed to sell on the proceeds, if I followed the cold chain and other legislation. This is far less onerous than setting myself up as a business that produces venison in unlimited quantities. I may then be able to penetrate markets that would not normally purchase venison by presenting a professionally produced and packaged product at a lower price than offered at the supermarket.

What then for the Scottish estates and professional stalkers countrywide, partly relying on the sale of venison carcasses at historically low prices? Are my small efforts scalable for these larger businesses?

Will stalking leases continue to rise in price, or will they maintain their relatively high cost, given that one way or another the deer population will decline in the UK? The retention of the stalker in the longer term is a factor. There are more licensed hunters than ever before, but if my experience is typical, many will pass through, shoot some deer and move on to another interest. I had some twenty-two years of gadget-free stalking, I loved it, and I loved the countryside it was carried out in. The last three years this has not been so, due largely to the technology available. It is both a blessing and a curse!

The 2020s are going to be an interesting decade.

End Notes

INTRODUCTION

[1] https://www.gov.uk/government/news/five-steps-motorists-should-take-to-avoid-deer-collisions-this-autumn 25/10/2018.

[2] http://www.thedeerinitiative.co.uk/pdf/contraception-and-wild-deer-control.pdf

[3] 'Potential role of contraception in the management of wild deer', printed in *Deer* magazine by Peter Green BVSc Cert EO MRCVS Veterinary Consultant.

[4] DEFRA, UK slaughter statistics, March 2020; BDS estimates.

CHAPTER 1

[1] https://basc.org.uk

[2] https://www.bds.org.uk

[3] http://www.hse.gov.uk/risk/controlling-risks.htm

CHAPTER 2

[1] 'The only limitation to skill in marksmanship is that imposed by the rifle and its ammunition. If a rifle and its cartridge are highly accurate, the shooter will take greater pride in the arm, he will shoot it more, his marksmanship will improve, he will get more game, he will win more matches. On the other hand, if the rifle is not accurate, the shooter gets nowhere with it, he does not develop into a good shot, he loses interest, and he soon disposes of it. Only accurate rifles are interesting.' Colonel Townsend Whelen, *American Rifleman* magazine, April 1957, p.46.

CHAPTER 3

[1] British Deer Society distribution survey. https://www.bds.org.uk/index.php/research/deer-distribution-survey

CHAPTER 4

[1] Gino J. D'Angelo *et al* (2007) 'Hearing Range of White-Tailed Deer as Determined by Auditory Brainstem Response', *The Journal of Wildlife Management*, Vol. 71, No. 4.

CHAPTER 7

[1] A. H. Kirton & E. G. Woods (1977) 'Blood weights and bleeding times of electrically stunned sheep slaughtered by three different procedures', *New Zealand Journal of Agricultural Research*, 20:4, 449–451.

[2] Gracey's *Meat Hygiene*, 11th edition, 2015, efficiency of bleeding, pp.152/3. Wiley Blackwell.

CHAPTER 8

[1] *The Wild Game Guide*, issued by the Food Standards Agency, Business Guidance. https://www.food.gov.uk/business-guidance/wild-game-guidance

CHAPTER 9

[1] https://www.gov.uk/government/collections/notifiable-diseases-in-animals

[2] **Reporting a notifiable disease**

In England, DEFRA Rural Services Hotline should be called, having all the relevant details to hand on 03000 200 301, choose the APHA (Animal and Plant Health Agency) option.

In Wales, the number is 0300 303 8268.

Scotland has various Field Service Offices:

    Ayr 03000 600703

    Galashiels 03000 600711

    Inverness 03000 600709

    Inverurie 03000 600708

    Perth 03000 600704

The general Scottish email address is alpha,scotland@apha.gov.uk

[3] https://www.ars.usda.gov/research/publications/publication/?seqNo115=337278

'Passage of scrapie to deer in a new phenotype upon return passage to sheep'

CHAPTER 10

[1] https://publications.parliament.uk/pa/cm201617/cmselect/cmenvfru/619/61905.htm Parliamentary business, Forestry in England, Woodland planting and management, March 2017

[2] www.WoodlandsTrust.org.uk, How trees fight climate change

[3] http://datazone.birdlife.org/userfiles/file/hunting/HuntingRegulations_Czech_Rep.pdf

[4] 2016 National Survey of Fishing, Hunting, and Wildlife-Associated Recreation, p.34.

[5] Sainsburys (2019) *Future of Food Report*, by the Department 22 agency.

[6] http://beefandlamb.ahdb.org.uk/market-intelligence-news/eu-medium-term-outlook-2018-2030/Beef consumption in the EU is expected to resume a downward trend, gradually declining from 11kg per capita in 2018 to 10.4kg per capita in 2030.

[7] https://www.farminguk.com/news/campaign-to-boost-british-venison-amid-fall-in-demand_56446.html

Index